BORN FIGHTER

Dedicated to my teacher, Keinosuke Enoeda Sensei.
You are guiding me still.

ACKNOWLEDGEMENTS

Thank you to all the very special people and their families who have shown me love, warmth and support over the years:

Mick Dewey, Aidan Trimble, Jess and Vanessa Lavender, Richard LaPlante, Ronnie Ross, Phil Owen, Jeff and Chris Westgarth, Andy and Julie Marsh, Mike O'Brien, Dave Cox, Dave Robinson, Billy Higgins, Bob Rhodes, Ticky Donovan, Alan Dalton, Will Davies, Paul Bonett, John Bowen, Jim Lewis, June Field, Franco Gianotte, Mick Shea, Steve and Val Ellis, Ian and Sue Gregory, Craig Raye, Kevin Slaney, Dolina Ross, Dave Scourfield, Lucy and Matt Bell, Simon Oliver, Cliff Hepburn, Malcolm Phipps, Simon Staples, Bob and Joy Waterhouse, Mark Elliott, Jeff Barwick, Owen Murray, Paul and Ann Walton, Fash Ghiaci, Iain and Paula Jefferson, John Heaton, Don Fullarton, Mick Billman, Chico Mbakwe, Paul Watson, Bo Channon, Richie Condon, Mike Dinsdale, Steve Quinn, Juli Pops, Ady Gray, Anna Parkin, Graham Palmer, Paul Herbert, Mike Hogan, Shari Bassiri, Fash Fay Omid and Kian Nasirpour, Bahram AgaAliyan, Stuart and Lesley Dykes, Shaun Banfield and Emma Robins.

Chris and his lovely Mairi.

Mum, Ben, Janice and Tracey.

A special thank you to Bernard Rose Photography for the photos of Enoeda Sensei and others.

CONTENTS

PART 2: ENOEDA SENSEI'S STUDENT, 1970–1977

PART 3: RONIN, 1978–1985

PART 4: SENSEI, 1986–2003

PREFACE

I would like to thank all those who have enriched my life, many of whom – but far from all – are mentioned in this book. Special thanks must go to Guru Chris Parker, without whose integrity, guidance and writing skill I would not even have considered this. Most importantly, thank you to my family, who have stood by me and supported me always.

What follow are just scenes from my life – episodes that have moulded me into who I am today. Please believe me when I say I could have filled this book three times over, but I have kept it short and sweet, to give you a smile or two and an insight into how I've lived.

I have tried to be as accurate as possible but, given the many bangs in the head I've received and the amounts of vodka I've consumed over the last fifty-four years, some dates and events may be a little off, so, please, give me a bit of leeway. After all, it's been a busy life...

Dave Hazard

'I am not a hard man or a great fighter, but I can and will fight if I have to.'

ONE CHANCE

I'm a martial artist. I earn my living teaching karate. I practise every day.

My teacher was one of the greatest martial artists of all time. His name was Keinosuke Enoeda. He was nicknamed 'The Tiger' and I'll tell you more about him later. One of the most important things he taught me is that you have to do everything as if you've got only one chance to get it right. And, if you think about it, that is all you have.

Just one chance.

It doesn't matter who you are or what you do, if you want to be good you have to practise so you can take that one chance.

You've probably heard the saying, 'Practice makes perfect'. Well, I don't know whether practice can make anything perfect, but you would think it would make you

1

better, wouldn't you? The more you do something, the better you get. That's obvious, isn't it?

No!

If you just do something, it won't make you better. If you do something with thought and understanding, you may get close to performing it well.

Performing well is OK when there's no pressure, but what about under duress? If you are to perform well under duress, your reactions have to be instinctive. If they're not, you miss your one chance and you fail. Simple as that. Thing is, in most situations if you miss your one chance your life still goes on. You might be upset or angry, or have other people upset or angry at you, but at least you have the opportunity to try again.

Miss your one chance in a fight without rules and you can be dead.

I came to realise very early on, and it has been reaffirmed many times in my life, that, when it comes down to the nitty-gritty, you have just one chance when it really, really counts.

In a conflict, even if you're the best fighter, you still have only one chance to make your superiority tell. If you don't take that chance, the other guy suddenly has one chance to get you! In those situations, one chance can be measured in fractions of a second – you don't have time to think. That's why I practise every day.

The stories that follow – the ones I've decided to share with you – are real and honest and true. In many ways my life will be very different from yours. In one way, though, it's exactly the same.

When push comes to shove, we've both got only one chance!

PART 1

AUDREY'S BOY
1952-1969

Chapter 1

MY BEST FRIEND

I was born on 4 March 1952 in St Andrew's hospital, Bow, East London. I was the first child of David and Audrey Hazard. They were East End folk. My Mum's family, the Nicholsons, worked in the docks. My Dad's parents owned a haulage company and, at one time, a pub. My Mum has five sisters and a brother. My Dad has two sisters. It wasn't all women, though. There were lots of really strong men in the family, too.

The Nicholsons were well known in the East End. My Grandad, Fred Nicholson, was the head of the family. He worked in the docks painting ships and, at weekends, he was the pot man in the Festival Arms in Poplar. They didn't have bouncers in pubs in those days. They had a pot man. His job was to say 'time's up' at the end of the night and then collect all the glasses. If someone didn't want to drink up quickly enough, the pot man's other job was to sort it. My Grandad's famous saying was, 'Door or window?'

He wasn't a big bloke. He was about five foot eleven but with a bull neck, arms like Popeye's and a right hand like a hammer. Many a time, as a kid, I would sit in the car park opposite the Festival Arms and watch blokes who'd been a bit saucy come out through the window. Even though he died when I was only eleven years old, I learned a lot from Fred Nicholson. I was given his name, too. His and my Dad's. I was christened David Frederick Hazard.

When we left hospital Mum and me went home to 6 Tomlins Terrace in Stepney. It was a two-up, two-down terraced house that had been split in half. We rented the top two rooms and shared an outside loo. We had a cooker on the landing, a bedroom, which we all used to sleep in, and a lounge with a couple of chairs and a Bakelite TV. As a little 'un I used to sit there watching Andy Pandy and Rag, Tag and Bobtail.

And that was our home. When I was four we had a kitchen put in, but before that we'd often go round to my Nan's, which was a forty-minute walk, to eat our meals or have a bath.

When I was five I started at Salmons Lane school, just round the corner from our house. That was where I had my first ever school photo taken. What a laugh! You see, when I was a baby, Mum used to put a bit of sugar on the end of my dummy to keep me happy. I loved it so much that, in the end, Mum put a dish of sugar in my cot so I could help myself. As I grew up, Nan used to give me a piece of pork fat or beef fat to suck on while we were waiting for dinner. You can guess what happened. By the time I was old enough for the school photo, I didn't have any teeth left! It didn't bother me. I just sat there in front of the camera with a big smile on my face. All you could see were gums!

The photographer must have felt really sorry for me, because when we got the photo back he'd managed to paint in loads of teeth. Mum went up the wall. She stormed off to the photographer's saying, 'My son hasn't got any teeth, so I don't want him to have any in the photo!'

I remember, as I got older, there were a few occasions when the local bobby marched me home. He'd knock on our front door and when Mum answered he'd say, 'Is this yours?'

'Yes,' my Mum would say, 'that's mine.'

The bobby would nod and frown. 'Well, he's been playing up.'

Then it was Mum's turn to frown. She'd send me inside. 'I'll see you in a minute,' she'd say.

'I'm thinking of taking him and locking him up,' the bobby would say, making sure that he was loud enough for me to hear. 'And I'm thinking of not letting you have him back!'

'I'll make sure he's good from now on,' Mum would promise.

Meanwhile, I was inside thinking, Oh my God! He's going to take me to prison and throw away the key!

Of course, Mum was never going to let anyone take me away. She was always fiercely protective of her children – willing to do whatever was necessary to keep us safe and help us grow. She had the sort of courage that can only grow out of a mother's love and, if the situation demanded it, she would be as brave as a lion for her children. That said, she was not a large woman. Mum was nothing like your stereotypical East End fishwife. She was a pretty lady, only five foot three tall and eight stone in weight. She was a beautiful woman – a class act – and, apart from being the best Mum in the world, as the years passed she was to become my best friend.

Chapter 2

AN ANGEL ARRIVES

My first sister, Janice, was born when I was six. She was, and is, an angel. She was born on a Tuesday, just like me and our younger sister, Tracey. We're all Tuesday's children!

I remember Mum coming home from the hospital with Janice, and seeing her sitting in the bedroom with this tiny baby in her arms. She was trying to keep them both cosy in front of a little electric fire that wasn't big enough to warm your arse.

I went over and said, 'Can I have a look?'

She said, 'Yeah, have a look.' But once I'd had a peek she told me, 'Now go over there and play with your toys.'

I was really disappointed. I felt as if she were saying, 'Now you've got a sister you've got to go and play on your own and leave her with me.'

I didn't realise at the time how tired and worried Mum

must have been. After all, she'd got a six-year-old son and a babe in arms to look after with only two rooms to live in and a cooker on the landing! The next day, though, everything was brilliant again. Mum gave me a big cuddle, saying, 'Come and hold your sister. Now what shall we all do together?'

One of the things we often did was go to Grandad Fred's. He had a little black mongrel dog called Nigger. Now, I know that this is an offensive word today, but back then it wasn't meant like that at all. Whenever Mum took Janice and me to visit, Grandad would send the dog home with us to make sure we arrived safely. This was a good forty minute walk, from Bath Street to Tomlins Terrace, and Nigger went with us all the way. He'd been doing it since I was a baby. Sometimes Mum would get on a bus and he would jump on after her. The conductor would ring the bell and tell Mum to get him off because dogs weren't allowed on buses. Once in a while, when I was still in my pram, Mum would go into a shop and Nigger would stay outside protecting me. If anyone came too close, he'd growl and warn them off. Once he'd followed us home, he'd turn round and go straight back to Grandad Fred's. That way Grandad knew that everything was all right.

To be honest, he didn't have much to worry about because everybody knew everybody in the East End. All the families had been there for ever. Even people in the Chinese community, which was quite strong at that time, were well known. The top woman in the Chinese community was called Joycie Farmer. She ran the New Friends Chinese restaurant.

When I was seven, my cousins Terry and Stephen and

me slipped in there on the quiet. Joycie recognised me straightaway.

She said, 'You're Audrey's boy' – and gave us some chicken chow mein and curry sauce.

We left Stepney when I was seven. My Dad's businesses were going well, so he decided we'd move for a better life. I wasn't too happy about it because I didn't want to leave my best mate, Richard. Mum tried to cheer me up by telling me that there'd be another boy called Richard at my new school. As it happened there wasn't, but there were quite a few dicks! Anyway, we moved to Harlow, which was a new town.

New town?

It felt more as if we were going to the other side of the planet, even though we were only forty minutes away from the East End. Mind you, when we arrived I thought we'd moved into a mansion. Our new house had two inside toilets, a bathroom, a kitchen, and enough bedrooms for everyone. We even had a garden! This was like something from *To the Manor Born* compared with Tomlins Terrace.

Janice and I had some great times at our new home. When she was two, she had a little pair of red Wellington boots, which she called 'Boodle Bashers' because she wore them to keep her feet safe from beetles and spiders. The problem was, she couldn't say the word beetle properly. The closest she could get was boodles, so her nickname became Boo.

As Janice got older, she started following me around the house more and more. She just loved to spend time with her big brother, and most of the time I loved it too. We even used to have silly wrestling matches together – not that we ever hurt each other. We'd watch the wrestling on TV, people like Mick McManus and Bert Royal, then we'd make up names for ourselves and leap and roll around the floor pretending to be wrestlers.

When I needed to be on my own, I'd make up a game to keep her busy for a while. Once, when she was four years old, I told her that she ought to hide in the cupboard at the top of my wardrobe just to show me how clever she was. She thought it was a great idea, so I gave her a leg up, shut the door and left her for a couple of hours. I had some time to myself and she lay there like a little mouse because her big brother had told her to.

Janice grew up to be a beautiful, intelligent and principled woman. She's had more than her share of health problems, which have deprived her of a lot of things in life, but she's never, ever complained. It's pissed me off, though. For a long time I blamed the Big Bloke upstairs for being such a bastard to my baby sister. Someone said to me once, 'If you dropped dead what would be the first thing you'd do? Would you go to heaven and train with all the famous martial artists of the past?' 'No,' I replied. 'I'd ask God if he could fight, and if he could he'd get it straight in the bollocks!'

I've changed my mind slightly over the years, because Janice has coped with everything so well, and when Mum nearly died (which happened twice) I found God again. I just gave everything up to him and said, 'Sorry, God. Do you want your balls back? I'll love you again and I won't fight you if you make her live for me.'

Thankfully, Mum pulled through and Janice continues to be a most special lady. The truth is, when I think of all the lovely people in my family and all the other wonderful people I've known, I've been truly blessed. I've had a few problems of my own, which we'll get to later, but nothing compared with some people. So I really have no reason to fight God any more.

I still can't understand, though, why he's treated one of his angels in the way he has.

Nan and Grandad Hazard were two of the lovely people in my life. Grandad was a very gentle, clever man, although I think he could be a bit heavy if he needed to be. As I've said, he was a haulage contractor and owned a pub. When I was still a baby, less than a year old, Nan and Grandad used to put me on the bar so I could dance. They'd dip their fingers in the Guinness and let me lick it off because, as the ads used to say, 'Guinness is good for you'. If I had a tummy ache as a kid they'd give me a little whisky and pep to sort it out. If it was cold in the morning they'd put a drop of brandy in my tea to warm me up on the way to school. It all sounds crazy now, but back then people didn't know there was any harm in doing things like that. My family loved me to bits and their intentions were always good.

Nan and Grandad Hazard used to take me down to Southend in their A40 Austin van. They'd sit in the front and I'd sit in the back on about four cushions and a blanket. We had some great days. They used to take me to Uncle Tom's Cabin, which was the place to go to buy tricks and treats. I'd make sand pies on the beach and then they'd buy me fish and chips. Once when I was there I bought a plastic flick knife. I thought it was fantastic and played with it all the way home. By the time we'd reached Harlow, I'd broken the spring. I still had my bucket and spade, though.

When I started at my new school in Harlow I got some stick straightaway because I was a London boy. Still, I was used to fighting and there was something more significant than a playground scuffle happening at home. Things weren't right between my Mum and Dad. They tried to hide it of course, but kids aren't daft. Mum was always there and Dad wasn't.

After a couple of years, Mum packed some things and off we went. Her marriage was over. Now you've got to understand that, in 1965, women didn't get divorced. For Mum to pack her bags and walk out with us was a very, very brave thing to do. Mind you, it wasn't only the men in the Nicholson family who were strong. The women were, too. They were all mentally very tough. Mum took us back to the East End and, although the family supported her, she still had to have the courage to do it.

Mum moved us into a flat in Leyton. Janice and I had our own bedroom and Mum slept on a pull-you-down in the lounge. During the day, she worked in a dry cleaner's. She worked in a factory. She'd do all sorts. She was always there before we went to school, and she was always there when we came home. In between, she worked all the hours God sent. She is, and has always been, a woman of sacrifice.

The school I went to was called Ruckholt Manor Secondary. It was big, old, dark-grey place with lots of power to it. At Ruckholt you could learn the four Rs. They were reading, 'riting, 'rithmetic and having a row. I was pretty good at all four, but guess which one I got to practise the most?

Chapter 3

A DOUBLE DIAMOND
WORKS WONDERS

The scrapping got more serious at Ruckholt for two reasons. I was getting older and I wouldn't join a gang. What happened was, I walked into the second-year class and the teacher said, 'Where do you want to sit?'

There was a group of boys going, 'Come over 'ere! Over 'ere!'

On the other side of the room there was a group of lads going, 'No! Come over 'ere!'

As for me, though, typical silly bollocks, I thought, I know where I'll sit: I'll sit in the middle with all the birds. That'll do me.

And I did. Which meant that, because I wasn't in either gang, I got a good hammering from both of them. That's the price you pay for being an individual.

One day, a group of them took me outside and gave me such a good kicking that I had to roll under a parked car to save myself. When I went home, Mum looked at the marks on my face and said, 'You lost that one.'

In the evening, when I was cleaning my teeth, I had my shirt off and Mum saw that my body was bruised and red. She said, 'It wasn't one person who did that.'

I said, 'No, it was a group.'

She said, 'Would you fight them one at a time?'

I said, 'Yeah.'

She said, 'Do you know where they live?'

I said, 'Yeah.'

She took me by the hand. 'C'mon, then,' she said, and we went round to their houses one at a time. Mum knocked on the door and explained to whoever answered why we were there. Most of the parents fell over with shock because we'd gone into their backyard and challenged them. I know now that Mum's approach gave us the psychological edge.

Anyway, we sorted all of them and the gangs at school never tried to pick on me again. In fact, a lot of people gravitated towards me because they knew that I didn't take any crap from anyone, and I didn't take any liberties, either. I learned that from my Mum. I was fourteen at the time.

The biggest problem I had at school was that I always looked like a posh boy. Even though I had only two shirts, Mum made sure I looked as smart as I could. Every night she hand-washed a shirt and polished my shoes. I used to scuff them on purpose, because I didn't want to look too smart. I must confess that, even though Mum made sure I was always clean and immaculately dressed, I was never the perfect pupil.

For example, I remember borrowing a car once from

one of the teachers. She was a Geography teacher, a lovely woman. When I say I borrowed her car, I didn't actually ask her if she would lend it to me. I found her keys on her desk and some of my mates and me thought we'd go for a joyride.

I drove it down the road in third gear because it was the only gear I could find. The problem was, when I stopped I couldn't turn it round because I couldn't get it in reverse. We had to leave the car and tell her what we'd done. Nowadays they'd get the police in for something like that. Back then, she took it as a giggle. She knew we meant no harm and just told us off. Some of the other teachers, though, took a different approach.

My Drama teacher, Mr Tyler, was the first person to buy me a pint. Well, it wasn't actually a pint it was a bottle of Double Diamond. What happened was, I'd been a nightmare in his class. In those days I thought Drama was for Marys, so I took the pee every chance I got. Eventually he'd had enough and made me stay after class.

He said, 'Right, Hazard, you think you're handy?'

I said, 'No.'

He said, 'I know you like to fight. Do you want to fight me?'

I couldn't say no, so I said, 'Yeah, if you like.'

Well, he gave me such a good hiding! He blacked my eyes and everything. Mind you, I deserved it.

Anyway, I went home and my Mum said, 'I hope they look worse than you do. Are you all right?'

I said, 'Yeah, no problem.'

The next day I went back to school and this kid came up to me and said, 'The Drama teacher wants to see you at break.'

I thought, Oh, shit! because I figured he was going to hit me again. Still, I went to see him and he said, 'Where's your Mum?'

I told him the truth. 'The last time I saw her she was ironing.'

He squinted at me, as if he wasn't sure whether I was trying to be awkward. 'Did you tell her I hit you?'

'No.'

He nodded. 'Right. You'd better come back and see me at lunchtime.'

When I heard that, I thought I was going to get another beating. I was sweating all morning thinking about how to duck his punches.

When I met him, he said, 'C'mon,' and started walking out of the building. Then I knew I was in even more trouble! I followed him, thinking, My God! He's taking me to the car park, so I'm really gonna get it this time! But I was wrong. He didn't hit me. Instead, he drove us to a pub about a mile and a half away.

Once we were inside, he said, 'You've acted like a man so I'm going to treat you like a man. What do you want to drink?'

I had no idea. Then I remembered the advert on the telly that went 'A Double Diamond works wonders, works wonders'. So I said, 'I'll have half of Double Diamond.'

He had a pint of bitter and we talked about my behaviour at school and the fact that I had bit of intelligence, so why didn't I use it? Then he said, 'Right, away you go.'

I said, 'Can't I have another one?'

He said, 'No, you can't.'

He made me walk back to school, too. And that was that. Mr Tyler was a great guy. He never had to hit me again and he never bought me another drink.

Chapter 4

'THERE'S A FELLA AT THE GATE'

Another really good teacher I had was Mr Nicholas. He was the Deputy Head, a Welshman, and an absolutely lovely man. He was old then, a heavy smoker, a bit of a drinker and as hard as nails. He was an ex-commando and, boy, could he handle himself!

He helped my Mum out a couple of times when the Headmaster had come to the end of his tether with me. He also used to cane me every Friday. As I said, I wasn't a perfect pupil. Mr Nicholas got so fed up with seeing me during the week that he told me just to turn up at four o'clock on a Friday and report how many strokes I needed. Of course, I used to lie. He'd see through it, though, and then I'd tell him the truth and take the full amount.

One day another lad and me were both sent for the cane at the same time. It was this lad's first caning and I thought to myself, I can have a bit of fun here. So I told him that if he put carbolic soap on his palms it wouldn't hurt as much. He was really grateful and rushed to the loos before we were called into the office. Mr Nicholas saw the soap on his hands and looked at me in a way that said, 'I know what you've done, Hazard, and we both know this will hurt him far more than it should.' Then he caned him just as hard as he did everyone else. The lad's tears came out horizontal!

I found out that Mr Nicholas could handle himself because of a lad called Andy Rogers. Andy Rogers ran Ruckholt Manor. He was probably too old to have been at school, but he'd decided to stay and nobody had asked him to leave. It made good sense to me. You see, the teachers didn't control the school, Andy Rogers did. He kept order. Each year had its own entrance gate. Each gate was looked after by the toughest lads in the year, picked by Andy. As the pupils came in they were asked to hand over some of their dinner money or sandwiches. We'd collect it all in, Andy would take his share, and then, at break time, we'd sell the sandwiches back to the kids who'd given them to us in the first place.

One day I was at our gate and these two fellas in their twenties turned up. One of them had a real edge to him. He was looking to hit a lad I didn't know, and when he realised that he wasn't going to find that particular lad he said, 'OK. Who's the hardest boy in the school?'

I said, 'Andy Rogers.'

He said, 'Right, bring him out here and I'll give him a good hiding instead.' This fella looked like a lump, but I knew Andy could fight like a demon, so I went straight to him.

He was sitting on a little wall outside the metalwork

room, reading the horses. 'Andy,' I said, 'there's a fella at the gate and he wants to clump the hardest bloke in the school.'

Andy closed his paper and was past me like that – click! No messing around. He didn't ask me what the fella looked like, or whether he was on his own. Nothing like that. He just went, 'Really?' And he was on his way.

As soon as I saw that, I thought, I want that commitment, that belief.

See, I'd always sort of had the attitude that said, If there's a problem, just deal with it. Only I had that because of fear. For me it was a case of go straight in and don't give yourself too much time to worry about it. If you lose, you lose. If you win, you win. Just get on with it. Andy had total control of his fear and I loved it.

He walked straight up to this fella and while the bloke was saying, 'Are you the –' he went smack! Split his eye wide open and it was game over. Then this fella's friend pulled out a blade. Before he could do anything with it, Mr Nicholas came over. In a split second, he'd covered the guy, bent him over, locked his arm, taken the knife and put it to the guy's throat!

'Don't be a silly boy,' he said as if he were talking to a first-year kid. 'You just stand over there and I'll speak to you in a minute.'

Then he told Andy to stop beating the first bloke, who was just a blubbering mess on the floor by that time. Mr Nicholas took charge of everything, called the police and sorted the situation. He was as calm as you like. Afterwards, even Andy said, 'Did you see that old guy move?'

We were all well impressed.

Another time, one of the teachers, a guy with a really violent temper, clumped a kid so hard round the head that the boy lost the sight in one of his eyes. It came back again later, but we didn't know it would.

Two of the older boys decided that the teacher needed to be taught a lesson. His classroom was on the second floor, so they went up there one lunchtime and threw him out of the window. One minute we're all standing in the playground and the next minute we're running for cover. I mean, fuck me, 'Is it a bird? Is it a plane? Nope, it's an English teacher!'

He broke his legs and his hips and was in hospital for six or seven months, but he never pressed charges.

Chapter 5

THE BIGGEST JOCKEY
IN THE WORLD

I rode a bike to school most days, but one particular morning I made the mistake of upsetting Mum with some backchat and she decided that, as my punishment, I should leave my bike at home and walk instead.

I thought, Fuck it! I'll have to run to school now. And then, to make matters worse, I remembered that my mates were waiting for me outside on their bikes. That was all I needed to help me make a stupid decision. I would ignore what Mum had said and go on my bike regardless. After all, I reasoned, she's still in her nightdress and dressing gown, so she can't possibly come after me.

I slammed the door as I left, carried my bike downstairs – we were living on the first floor at the time – and jumped on it as I greeted my mates. They didn't respond as they usually did. They were all too busy staring behind me, their eyes opening wide in disbelief. I looked over my shoulder and saw Mum rushing towards me, her gown flowing behind her. What happened next was like one of those horrible dreams in which you are trying to run, but can never quite get going. As Mum flew towards me I turned the pedals, straining to gain some momentum, but it all seemed to be taking far too long! I pedalled harder and faster and, just as I thought that I might be able to get away, Mum reached out and caught hold of the back of the saddle with one hand.

'I told you,' she said. 'You're walking to school today!'

My mates just took off, leaving me alone, watching my Mum, in her dressing gown, marching my bike back into the flat.

I don't know when Mum started courting, but I was fifteen when I first met Ben. He came from Walthamstow originally. He was a good horse rider and had wanted to be a jockey, but he got too big. The truth is, when you're six foot tall and fourteen stone, of muscle you're never going to be a jockey.

When I first met Ben he owned a grocer's shop in Brentwood, Essex. Later, he worked as a labourer on the roads. He worked like a Trojan and was known on the council as 'Ben the Man' because he was always honest and straight. That's just the way Ben is. No one ever made a road that was as straight as Ben the Man. Anyway, Ben came to our home and was introduced to us, and I knew Mum was asking us, 'Is this OK? And if it's not then he's gone.' You see, nothing mattered to her more than her children.

I guess it must have been really challenging for Ben. He must have known he'd got only one chance to get it right. Thing is, though, he's a class act. He was very calm, very strong. We got to know him gradually, over time, and it soon became obvious that he made Mum happy. That was good enough for me. Besides, I liked listening to him, and I liked the strength around him. Ben became my hero and that hasn't changed. To be honest, when Ben joined us it took some of the weight off my shoulders. I was a fifteen-year-old lad who could swagger a bit. Ben was a real bloke who could handle any problem.

Mum and Ben married in a register office just around the corner from where we lived. It was a wonderful day. My Nan was there, God rest her soul, and all my aunts and uncles. The only one missing was Grandad Fred. He'd died in 1963 from thrombosis. He was only fifty-eight. This strong, dignified man, who used to put his arms out to the sides and have two of my cousins swinging on one arm and me and Janice swinging on the other, died so young. He'd never given me much direct advice, but he had taught me a lot about how to behave as a man. For example, if he didn't like how I was behaving he'd just look at me in a certain way and I'd go, 'Hmm, this isn't the right thing to do, then.' And I'd stop.

The kids in the family weren't allowed to go to Grandad Fred's funeral, but Terry and me had no intention of missing it. We bunked off school and sat in this block of flats watching the procession go by. It was massive. There were loads of cars. I couldn't believe how many there were. Terry and me watched this fantastic tribute to an amazing man without saying a word. We just sat there and cried.

Although I'd lost my Grandad, I'd now got Ben as my stepdad. Once Mum and Ben were married we moved to a flat in Livingstone College Towers. We were on the seventh floor and the flat was great. Nowadays, people talk about tower blocks and go, 'Ooh! Ooh!' as if they're hell on earth, but we were in heaven. You see, no matter where we lived, Mum always made sure that we were washed and clean, that we had food and, most of all, that we had lots of love. You can't beat that.

Ben didn't encroach whenever Mum had to deal with me for misbehaving. He was always there, though, waiting for his cue if she ever needed him. He was Mr Cool. Usually the most he'd do was just give me a little look. There was only one time that he got really pissed off with me, and that was my own fault.

We were sitting having dinner, and I was rude to Mum. I was a teenager, my hormones were raging, and I was being a little bastard to tell you the truth. Anyway, Ben had heard enough. He put his knife and fork down, grabbed me calmly by the throat, lifted me up as if I were a toy, raised his fist – which looked as big and strong as a hammer – and said very quietly, 'If you ever speak to your mother like that again, I'll punch your head off.'

Mum was in between us in an instant, saying, 'Ben! Put him down! Put him down! Don't touch him!'

'Fair enough,' he said. Then he looked at me and said, 'Don't ever do that in my earshot again, young man.'

I was staring at his fist, which looked about two feet wide, thinking to myself, If he fuckin' hits me with that, he's only gonna hit me once and it's all I'll need!

Ben didn't hit me then and he's never had to raise that fist to me again. He knows I love him to death, and it always makes me laugh when I think that he wanted to be a jockey. It's not that he's just too big to be a jockey, he's the biggest guy in the world.

Chapter 6

'I DON'T WANT TO BE A F*CKIN' HAIRDRESSER!'

I left school when I was sixteen. I think I actually left a couple of weeks earlier than I should have. I'd had some good times and some bad times at Ruckholt Manor, but overall I'd enjoyed being there. They've knocked it down now and replaced it with a Nissan garage. Good job all those cars weren't in the car park when I was fourteen...

Anyway, I think Mum panicked a bit when I told her I'd left. 'What are you going to do?' she asked.

It was a good question. I had a little part-time job in a men's hairdressers shop, where I used to sweep the floors and stuff, but I wasn't planning on working there full-time.

'Obviously you're not going to do anything with your mind,' Mum said. 'So it's going to have be with your hands. What about the hairdressers?'

I thought to myself, I don't want to be a fuckin'

hairdresser! They're all Marys! Which I found out later to be a complete load of bollocks. Some of the hardest blokes in the East End were hairdressers.

Thankfully, Mum took no notice of what I thought and got me an apprenticeship with a hairdresser called Dave Cox. Dave wasn't the owner, but he was the manager of the men's side and he took me on. The deal was £2.50 a week for a three-year apprenticeship followed by another two-year 'improver'. I thought, Yeah, this'll last about ten minutes but I'll give it a shot. Actually, it lasted a lot longer than that. Dave Cox became my first real mentor, apart from Ben, and he taught me loads of stuff about life.

Dave was twenty-six at the time – a bloke compared with me – and a phenomenal hairdresser. He is about six foot two tall, wiry, strong and good-looking. He was smart and quietly spoken, but you knew he was a handful. Most of all, he was a great teacher.

The place where we worked was an old-fashioned barber's shop with a women's hairdressers upstairs. Dave taught me how to shave a bloke by making me practise on a balloon. He'd blow it up, lather it, then give me a cutthroat razor to work with. My job was to shave the balloon without bursting it. If I'd been a bit saucy that day, he'd blow the balloon up really tight and, as soon as I touched it with the razor, bang! – I was covered in shaving cream.

We had a tailor's dummy in the back room – but it was a dummy of a woman, just the top half with hips, waist and a pair of breasts. I was already dating girls, so one day Dave said, 'Come here, boy. I'll show you what to do.'

He put a bra on the dummy and taught me how to undo it using only one finger and thumb. After a bit of practice I was able to do it with my eyes closed. (It's a skill I've never lost.) After that, I could put my hand up a girl's jumper and undo her bra so quickly she wouldn't even know it was undone. My hand would then go round the front and the girl's eyes would open up a bit as if to say, 'How did you do that?' Of course, I'd do my best to act cool.

Dave told me stuff that Ben, being my Dad, couldn't. He said, 'When you're with your girlfriend, you don't go in too quick. You kiss her first. You do this, you do that. You don't go straight to the honey pot.'

Although Dave knew lots more than I did, we still fooled around as mates. We both became interested in the martial arts at the same time. Once, we had a fight in the hairdresser's with these six-foot long bamboo poles. It was like a scene out of a samurai film. We were just battering each other when suddenly Dave jumped through a door and disappeared. He went round the side, got behind me and jabbed me in the back. I jumped round, swinging my pole, missed him and smashed a glass window. We had to come up with a really good story to explain that to the boss!

Another time, we were having this great fight, throwing anything and everything we could at each other. There was hair, scissors, all sorts of stuff being thrown around. Now, downstairs there was a cellar, and there was a hole in the floor of the room above it, so you could see into it. When the fight was over, I hid in the cellar and locked the door, thinking to myself, I'm staying in here, 'cos if I come out he'll get me again.

Dave is a very patient guy and I knew he'd be waiting for me. Well, I'm a stubborn bastard myself, so I thought, Right! I'll stay here as long as it takes.

So I stayed there. And stayed there. And time passed and I didn't move a muscle in case he heard me. Then, after about three hours I heard this creaking sound and I looked up and Dave was peering at me through the hole in the floor. He said, 'What the fuck are you doing there?'

I said, 'Hiding from you. I know you've been waiting for me.'

He said, 'You silly little fuck! I've been home, had a bath, had my tea. I've done all sorts.' He laughed his head off.

The funny thing is, I did end up being a good hairdresser. I worked hard at it and I loved it, because the rewards you got were great. I had mates who worked on the car line in Dagenham. They put wheels on cars, they put something else on, but they never saw the finished product. I did. Fifteen, maybe twenty, times a day I had the satisfaction of transforming a mop of hair into something that looked really good. I was so good at it that I used to earn more in tips than I did in my wages. In fact, even now I can still cut a good short head of hair better than most people.

Chapter 7

PRIM AND PROPER

Edie Nicholson was my Nan on my Mum's side. She was a tiny woman, barely over five foot tall, with grey hair. She always looked prim and proper, but she had a sense of devilment inside her.

She would often visit us at Livingstone College Towers, and then I'd take her home at about 9.30 at night. We'd get in the lift and I'd press the button for the ground floor. Nan would immediately press the buttons for some of the floors in between. When the lift stopped, Nan would rush out, press someone's doorbell, and then hurry back to me. If someone opened their front door before the lift closed, they'd see a seventeen-year-old lad standing next to a prim and proper old lady, who looked as if butter wouldn't melt in her mouth. She'd have an innocent look on her face, and that unbreakable kind of death grip that only old ladies use on their handbag.

Nan would look straight back at the other person, as if to say, 'You don't possibly think that it could have been this prim old lady, do you?' Then, as the door began to close, she'd look accusingly at me.

Some nights as we crossed the car park, she'd run past all the dustbins rattling the lids as she went – just to see how much noise she could make.

If you want to know where both my Mum and me got our mischievous sense of humour, I can tell you: it was Edie Nicholson. So don't blame me if you've ever been the victim of one of my jokes. I can't help it. It's in my genes.

Chapter 8

'I'VE JUST MET GOD ON LEGS!'

I've always been one for searching out new experiences, so, when I had a problem with the owner of the hairdressers, I moved on and worked in a number of different places. I stayed close friends with Dave throughout and eventually worked with him again once he'd got his own place. You've got to understand that guys didn't go to a proper East End barber's shop just to get their hair cut. Of course, they did want a damned good haircut, but they also came for a packet of three, a couple of shirts out of a box, and a few good jokes to take away with them.

For a time I worked in a hairdresser's owned by a guy called Johnny Swainsbury. He was a beautiful hairdresser, very meticulous. He'd built a pool room and a sauna at the back of the shop. The saucy fucker! Anyway, unfortunately for him, he had very bad arthritis and a big, ferocious-looking Doberman that wasn't worth spit as a guard dog. To be fair, that's not quite right. When Johnny was around you couldn't go near the dog without it growling and showing its teeth. Once he was out of the room, though, it became as silly as a pair of bollocks and you could do what you liked with it. Johnny lived in Essex and the shop was in Plastow in the East End. It was a rough area and the shop had been broken into a few times, so Johnny decided he'd leave the Doberman there overnight.

'That'll sort the fuckers out,' he said.

I told him that it wouldn't, that the dog was just silly when he wasn't around, but he took no notice. A few nights later someone broke into the shop. They stole a few of the usual bits and pieces – and they stole the dog as well! Johnny did get it back a few days later, but he never left it alone in the shop again.

It was while I working there that I met Ray Prince. I don't know what his day job was, but I do know that he worked the doors. One day he came into the shop with one of his hands bandaged up. I asked him how he'd done it and he said, 'Karate.'

I said, 'I've heard of that.' I'd read a book about it by a bloke called Bruce Tegner.

Ray told me that he trained at a club at Blackfriars and that there were Japanese instructors teaching. I said that I fancied having a go and he invited me down with him. I told Dave Cox, who said, 'I'll have some of that.' So we went together the next Thursday. It was August 1969. I didn't know then that my life was about to change for ever.

The class was in a church hall called John Marshall Hall. That first night, we walked in and maybe twenty-five people were already milling around. Ray introduced us to Ray Fuller, who was the club secretary and the senior grade – apart, of course, from the Japanese. You could tell just by looking at Ray that he was a hard bastard. He told us we could sit down and watch the class. The style of karate that was being taught was called Shotokan.

Everyone was warming up and there was an air of expectancy in the room. It was like, 'Hell, what's going to happen tonight?' I'd never seen anything like it.

The Japanese instructor who was in charge was called Enoeda Sensei. Actually his name was Enoeda Keinosuke (the Japanese put their surname first) and *Sensei* is a title that means 'teacher' or 'the one who has gone before'. When Enoeda Sensei called 'Line up!' everyone was there in a flash, like soldiers.

What happened then was all so focused and so deliberate. It was controlled violence like I'd never seen before. The class was just the usual mix of the three Ks: *kihon*, which are the basic techniques, *kata*, which are set forms, and *kumite*, which means sparring.

That night Enoeda Sensei was assisted by another Japanese instructor, Kato Sensei. The two of them demonstrated what they wanted the class to do, and slapped people in the stomach and tested their stances by seeing how easily they could move them out of position. The first time Enoeda Sensei kicked someone in the head I couldn't believe my eyes. I thought, Fuck me! What just happened there? You have to remember that this was 1969. Apart from a few books on karate, we hadn't seen it before. It would be a few more years before Bruce Lee appeared in our cinemas kicking and punching like a demon, so nothing had prepared me for what I watching. Until then, I thought that the only time you could kick someone in the head was after you'd knocked them down!

When you watched Enoeda Sensei you could see he was the Boss. When I heard him punch, the whole place seemed to move! I thought, I've just met God on legs!

I realised very quickly that these guys could teach me how to really scrap. I did know some good street fighters at the time, but they wouldn't teach you anything – other than giving you a few clumps. No one teaches you how to fight in the street. Apart from boxing and judo clubs, there weren't any other places to go to learn about structured fighting. That night I watched a yellow belt, I found out later that his name was Terry Eden and he was a former ABA boxing champion, and I thought to myself, That'll do! If I can get just as good as him I'll be chuffed! Little did I know that we'd end up taking our black belt exam together.

After the class, I looked at Dave Cox. He looked at me. I said, 'D'you fancy this?' He said, 'Yep!' So we asked Ray Fuller if we could join up. He said, 'Yeah.' Then he looked at me. 'You are eighteen, aren't you?' I said, 'Yeah. Sure.' It was only a little fib, because I was only six months away.

Ray then asked if we wanted a karate suit. We both did. We got a *Tokaido gi* – which is the dog's bollocks! – and a white belt for £2.50. At the time we thought that was a bit of a liberty. Now, of course, I know what a great price it was for such a quality suit.

I was only able to watch the next class, which was on

Monday, because my *gi* (karate suit) hadn't arrived. I started training the following Thursday. There we were, Dave and me as the new boys in the class. One of the other students showed us how to tie our belts. Enoeda Sensei showed us how to make a proper fist and how to do a front stance. Thirty-five years on I'm still practising what I learnt in that first class.

Two weeks later I found out that there were also classes on Tuesdays and Fridays at the *Budokwai*, a club in South Kensington. That meant I was able to train four nights a week. By then I was bitten by the karate bug. I'd been training for only a few weeks when one day I arrived at Blackfriars and was told by Ray Fuller that I couldn't train because there was a grading going on.

I said, 'Hold up. I've come all the way from the East End. What do they do in a grading?'

Ray said, 'They go up and down showing what they've been taught.'

I said, 'I'll have a go at that.'

Ray sighed and said, 'Go on, then. Give me your five bob.'

So I did. I took the grading and didn't have a clue! The *kata* we had to do was called *Heian Shodan*. My mind went into a blur. I remember thinking, This *kata* has got twenty-one moves and it's got knife hand blocks in it. So, while everyone else did the *kata* correctly, doing a mixture of punches, blocks and stances, I just did twenty-one knife hand blocks, going off in all directions. While the others tried to do it with military precision I was all over the place!

Enoeda Sensei stared at me in disbelief. When the *kata* was over, he pointed at me and said, 'You! Get off!'

I thought, Why won't he let me spar? And then, typical silly bollocks that I was, I decided that maybe it was because I was too good and didn't need to.

After the sparring everyone gathered round and Sensei read out the results. When he got to me, he tutted and said, 'Hazard! You stupid! Temporary pass.'

I said to Ray Fuller, 'What does he mean?'

He replied, 'He means that you've got no idea. I told you not to train tonight.'

Basically I'd just failed my first ever grading! You had to pass nine belts before you could try for black belt and I'd failed the very first one. Mind you, Enoeda Sensei never failed me again. I did, though, have a bit of trouble coming to terms with the etiquette required in a karate *dojo* – which is what you call the place where you train.

As I've already said, the instructors in those days used to come along and push you around a little bit – give you a knock to test your stance and stuff like that. In one class, Kato Sensei was coming down the line saying, 'Stance OK?'

Now, who's going to say 'no' to that? So, when he got to me, I said, 'Yes, Sensei.'

He just swept me off my feet and walked away. I suppose what happened next was pure instinct. I'd been taught in the East End that if someone put you on your bum you got up quick and gave them one back. So I jumped to my feet and lunged after him. He saw me coming and gave me an almighty back kick! I definitely wasn't rushing to my feet after that and, while I was recovering, Kato Sensei asked Ray what was wrong with me. Ray explained that I didn't understand the rules yet.

For the next three months I trained four nights every

week and at the next grading I went straight up to red belt. After another four months of training I passed yellow belt. I'd done it! I'd reached the belt I wanted to get to. However, by now I'd decided that I wanted to keep going until I was a green belt. You see, I was already being taught the *kata* – called *Heian Yondan* – that you had to do for green belt. I really liked it because it included chops and elbow strikes and knees to the head. An interesting thing is that, even to this day, when I'm asked what my favourite *kata* is I start by saying, 'Heian Yondan.'

When I was a yellow belt, I found out about the two-week summer course that was held every year at Crystal Palace. There was four hours of training every day, plus the chance to take a grading. The list of Japanese instructors present was just incredible. Apart from Enoeda Sensei, who was a sixth *dan* at the time, there was Kase Sensei, who was a seventh *dan*, Shirai Sensei, another sixth *dan*, three fifth *dans* – Miyazaki Sensei, Ochi Sensei and Asano Sensei – plus Kato Sensei, who was a fourth *dan*, and Sumi Sensei, who was third *dan*. Not surprisingly, hundreds of students attended.

I took every class for the full two weeks. I passed my green belt grading at the end of the first week and was amazed when Enoeda Sensei suggested that I try for my purple belt at the end of the second. Normally, we could grade only every three months but Sensei explained, 'One week at Crystal Palace is like three months anywhere else.'

So, I took the purple belt grading and passed that as well. It was strange to think that two weeks before at

Blackfriars, I'd been training as a yellow belt and now I was going back as a purple belt. The funny thing was, the only reason I'd had the confidence to go to Crystal Palace in the first place was that I'd learned some chops in Heian Yondan!

One night, during a class at Blackfriars, Enoeda Sensei said that it was important to perform what's known as the *kiai* when doing your best technique. A *kiai* is a yell – a spirit shout – that comes from the pit of the stomach. It can help strengthen your own technique and scare your opponent. When I heard Sensei say this, I thought, Right! I'll show him how hard I'm trying! And I *kiai*ed on every single technique I did. I went up and down the *dojo* three times, shouting like mad, until Sensei couldn't stand it any longer.

'Oi! You!' He shouted to me. 'Shut up!'

I thought, Fuck me! I was only trying to show you that I was doing my best.

You have to understand that I've never been the sort of person who likes to stand out from the crowd – unless I'm teaching or fighting, and then I really do want to be noticed. It was just that I was committed to doing whatever Enoeda Sensei wanted. As I said, it was clear from the beginning that he was the Boss and, although I was only a purple belt, I liked the idea that he was my Boss, too.

PART 2

ENOEDA SENSEI'S STUDENT
1970-1977

Chapter 9

'WHERE THE LAND LIES'

Ray Fuller was an inspirational karate man. He was strong and wiry, with a phenomenal attitude and spirit. He worked as a painter and decorator. One lunchtime, he went on to the roof of the building where he was working to practise *kata*. What he didn't know was that he was being watched by some office workers in the building opposite. They looked out of their window and saw this guy swinging his arms and legs about and jumping up and down. Since they'd never seen karate before they had no idea what he was doing and came to the conclusion that he was a madman. They promptly phoned the police and said that a lunatic was about to throw himself off a building.

The police, along with Ray's boss, raced to the site and rushed up to the roof, desperate to stop Ray from committing suicide. When he told them that he had no intention of killing himself and that he had simply been practising a *kata* called *Kanku-Dai,* which means 'to view the sky', the police thought it was hilarious. Unfortunately for Ray, his boss wasn't so amused and sacked him for time wasting!

Ray not only taught classes at Blackfriars when the Japanese Sensei were away, but also travelled to other *dojos* to teach. At that time there were only a couple of dozen black belts in the country and Ray was one of them. Consequently, he was well respected as an instructor in his own right. I was still only a purple belt when he asked me to go with him to a club in Portsmouth.

'It's a nice little group down there,' he said. 'There's a black belt called Phil Elliott and a couple of brown belts. One of them, a bloke by the name of Mick Dewey, is getting a bit above himself. I can't give him a clump, given that I'm the instructor, but you're a live spark and I thought that you could come with me and show him where the land lies.'

'Course I will,' I said. 'I'll have some of that.'

Unbeknown to me, about a week beforehand Ray had said to Mick Dewey, 'Listen, Mick, I've got this young kid up at the Blackfriars *Dojo.* He's just coming through the ranks but he's a bit of a cocky little sod and needs bringing down a peg or two. It's a bit hard for anyone at the *dojo* to clump him, so I'd like you to put him in his place.'

Mick had said, 'Yeah, no problem. Bring the little sod down and I'll sort him out.'

So, the scene was set. Ray's car back then was a 'Bond Bug'. It was like a super-charged three-wheeler Robin Reliant. Imagine a yellow wedge of cheese with plastic flaps instead of proper doors, two seats in the front and a shelf in the back and you've got the picture.

Ray's wife, Pauline, came along too. She sat in the front with him, which meant that I had to sit in the back on the shelf seat. That was bad enough, but what made it worse was the fact that I was sharing the seat with Ray's bloody great Doberman!

I'm not worried about dogs as a rule, but I wasn't happy at the thought of sitting next to that thing all the way from Blackfriars to Portsmouth. Still, there was nothing I could do about it, so I climbed in. The Doberman wasn't too sure about me and I certainly wasn't too sure about the Doberman.

After a few miles I realised that both the dog and I were sitting, unmoving, looking straight ahead. I turned my head to the right a little bit just to get a better look at him. He immediately turned his head to the left to look at me and growled – 'Grrrr!'

I didn't like that, so I straightened my head and looked to the front again. The dog did the same. That became our agreement. Four or five times during the trip I forgot and turned my head towards him. Each time he looked back at me and went, 'Grrrr!' I'd straighten my head, he'd straighten his and everything would be hunky-dory.

It only got really awkward when we stopped to have a drink and I had to get out, or when the dog would fart. Oh my God! It stank the car out! Of course, Ray would make out it was me. 'Is that you, you dirty little sod?' he'd say.

'No, it's your dog.'

'Don't you blame my dog now.'

Pauline just laughed, saying that whenever Ray farted he always blamed the dog.

Let me give you an idea of just how loony this animal was. Ray was driving round a bend one time, with the Doberman sitting next to him, when it saw another dog walking across the road. It was so keen to have a go at this other dog that it jumped straight out through the plastic flaps, knocking half its teeth out in the process!

It also got a boot from the Boss one night at Blackfriars *dojo*. Ray thought that Enoeda Sensei was away and that he was teaching the class. He had a habit in those situations of bringing the Doberman along with him and letting it loose in the hall before the class started. The dog would go mad, snapping and snarling as it raced in, and we would all run for the security of the stage at the far end of the hall. Fortunately, the floor was so well polished that the dog couldn't get a strong enough grip to jump up after us.

This particular night Ray got it wrong. Sensei was in the *dojo* and was just about to start the class when Ray opened the door without looking inside and released the Doberman. Everyone ran for the stage with the dog in hot pursuit. Everyone, that is, apart from one.

Enoeda Sensei just stood and watched the mayhem. The dog skidded to a halt in front of the stage and then realised that there was one person it could still attack. It charged at Sensei, who calmly kicked it in the ribs, knocking it back across the floor. At that point, Ray opened the door and came in. He was grinning, expecting to see us all cowering on the stage. When he saw Sensei in the *dojo* with a face like thunder and his dog squealing like a stuck pig his grin vanished. He turned and ran out of the *dojo*, with his dog scurrying after him. Sensei watched them go, then looked at us and said, 'So! You are all more afraid of the dog than you are of me!'

We all said, 'No, Sensei!' in unison.

It was a particularly hard session that night.

Anyway, when we arrived at the Portsmouth club, I changed quickly and went straight into the *dojo*. As soon as I made eye contact with Mick I realised that he was the guy I'd come to sort out. He stood out like a sore thumb. There are plenty of guys who can have a row when push comes to shove, but they still need to be shoved in the first place. Mick was clearly the sort who didn't need to be shoved. Well, that's why I was there!

Ray took us through a fairly normal class, then said, 'OK! Find a partner. Let's do some scrapping.'

Mick and I faced up, bowed and proceeded to knock several barrels of crap out of each other! I hit him with everything I'd got. He just laughed and came back with some corkers.

I thought, Who is this guy?

He was sticking straight kicks into my stomach and groin. I was trying to move off to the side and clump him in the face or kick him in the back of the neck. We had a bloody good scrap and by the end of it we were covered in lumps and bruises that neither of us was going to admit to.

Afterwards we went over to the local pub. I was at the bar when Mick walked in. He came up and stood by me.

I said, 'D'ya wanna drink?'

He said, 'No, I don't.'

I said, 'Please your fucking self.'

He nodded. 'Ray told me that you were a cocky little bastard and needed taking down a peg or two.'

I said, 'That's funny, 'cos he told me you had a bit of an edge to you, and needed sorting out.'

We looked at each other and then looked behind us. There was Ray, sitting in the corner holding his belly and laughing. We knew then that he'd set us up to have a good scrap.

Mick turned back to me and said, 'Tell you what, I will have that drink.'

So I bought him a drink, then he bought me one, and that was how our friendship began. It didn't take us long to get very close. We've always had a bond between us and, as the years have passed, it's got better and better. Now we're like brothers.

Chapter 10

A PRINCESS IS BORN

My youngest sister, Tracey, was born on 24 February 1970. She was a pretty little dream and everyone in the family doted on her. As she grew up, anything that Mum and Ben couldn't afford to buy for her, me and Janice did. We spoiled her rotten. She was our little princess and I became her hero.

One lunchtime, when Tracey was still a baby, I was driving her and Mum back from Walthamstow market in Dave Cox's car. He had an Austin 1100 with a very distinctive number plate – it had the letters 'POO' on it.

As I was making a left turn I slowed down to let a couple of pricks cross the road in front of me. They neither thanked me nor made any effort to hurry up – that's how I realised that they were pricks. Instead of showing some manners, they just sauntered across the road as if they'd got all the time in the world. I was on my lunch break and needed to get back to the barber's for the afternoon session, so I tooted the horn to hurry them along. They turned round and gave me the finger, calling me all the names under the sun. The red mist descended and I was out of the car like a shot!

I kicked the first guy in the chest, which was more than enough for him. Then I turned towards the other one, who was, by now, realising that he didn't have all the time in the world. He'd got no more idea how to fight than his mate. These were just two disrespectful, arrogant pricks – the soft variety rather than the hard. No matter, I'd got enough blood rushing to my head for all of us! I clumped the second guy and down he went.

It was only then that I heard a greengrocer who'd come out of his shop, shouting, 'Hold up! Hold up! He's killing them! He's killing them!'

By then Mum was by my side, with Tracey under her arm. She told me to get back in the car. I didn't need telling twice and we drove off, leaving the two guys in the middle of the road and the greengrocer shouting his head off.

That night, at the dinner table, Ben asked Mum how her day had been. She very deliberately didn't tell him about the fight. Just when I was thinking that he would never find out, Tracey chimed up in her baby voice, 'Dadey killed someone today, Dad! Dadey killed someone!'

So much for getting away with it! I told Ben what had happened, made it clear that no one had died, and then did my best to change the subject.

I did, though, get away with it as far as the police were concerned. You see, when I'd got to the barber's I told Dave Cox what had happened. Which was a good job, because when he went home that night he got a visit from the police.

'You attacked two men today,' the copper said.

Dave shook his head. 'No. I didn't.'

'It was your car that was being driven.'

'No, it wasn't. My car stops with me, and I've been in the barber's all day.'

The copper wasn't too impressed, but there was nothing he could do at that point, so he left.

Dave asked around a bit and found out who had reported the incident. Then he paid him a visit. When the guy opened his front door and saw Dave standing there, he didn't recognise him. Which, of course, was the point. Remember, Dave is six foot two tall, with a wiry build and very different features from mine. He was also wearing a long coat with the collar up.

Dave didn't waste any time. 'You've been complaining that I beat you up,' he said.

'It wasn't you,' the man replied.

'I know that,' Dave said. 'It wasn't my car either. My car is "POO".'

'That's what I saw on the number plate!' the man protested.

'Then you must have seen it wrong,' Dave told him in an authoritative manner. 'Because my car was with me all day. So I think you need to go back to the police and tell them you've made a mistake, don't you?'

The man realised that it would be an even bigger mistake to ignore Dave's request and withdrew his complaint. He may well have seen a car called 'POO', but I think he was close to shitting himself when Mr Cox made his presence felt!

When Tracey was six years old she asked me to teach her some karate moves. She'd grown up watching me come home with trophies and black eyes, and now she wanted her big brother to teach her how to kick and punch. I decided that it would be good to show her something that would help her out in the playground if she ever needed it – not that I ever thought she would!

I taught her a *mawashi-geri*, a roundhouse kick, which is something that young children, who are like bands of rubber, find easy to do. I showed her how to hold her hand in front of her face and then kick just beyond that point. I thought no more of it until Mum was called to school because Tracey had had an argument with a boy and kicked him in the face! From that moment on, Mum banned me from teaching any more karate to my little princess. Not that she's ever needed it. Why would she? She's always had me there.

Chapter 11

COMING OUT OF
THE CUPBOARD

I was a brown belt when I first went to national squad training. All my heroes were present, people like Terry O'Neill, Bob Poynton, Billy Higgins, Bob Rhodes, Steve Cattle and all the rest. I just looked at them and thought, I want to be among these! I want to test myself against them!

Now you have to realise that, at this point, I still had enough trouble at Blackfriars. I wasn't the cock of the *dojo* by a long way – I was just one of the young guns coming up through the ranks. So, there I was trying to get into the national squad and my eyes were all over the place, trying to steal things from my heroes. I'd see Terry O'Neill kick and say to myself, 'I want that!' I'd watch Billy Higgins sweep someone and feel the same.

The most senior grade in the class was Sensei Andy Sherry. He is not a man of enormous stature – actually he's smaller than I am – but his heart is bigger than his chest. He is as tough as nails, has a phenomenal spirit and a lightning-fast reverse punch that could nail anyone. I watched him zooming across the floor like a rocket and I thought to myself, He's coming to the end of his competition career. He's told everyone he's retiring. He's helping Enoeda Sensei out a lot more now. Sure, his punch is quick but I ain't too slow.

Which was true. I didn't have many gifts when it came to karate, but I did have very fast reactions. I was very quick, which was fortunate because there are no weight divisions in competition. If you are only five foot six tall you can fight someone who is six foot four tall and built like a brick shithouse. I actually liked that, because karate should equate to all shapes and sizes. You can't say to someone outside, 'Oh, you're a bit big for me – can you come back next week?' You deal with it.

Anyway, Enoeda Sensei took the class. We did some basics and a little bit of pair work and then it was time for sparring. Everyone sat down and the first one up, just to prove that he was the knob, was Sensei Sherry. The question was, who wanted to get up and fight him? All the experienced fighters there could probably have given him some trouble, but the tendency in these situations is for them to let the middle ranks test themselves.

Well, silly bollocks here had already made his decision. I wanted him! I jumped up instantly and rushed out to face him. I was probably the least able person in the *dojo*, but in my mind I was younger and faster, and I wanted it more. Boy, was Sensei Sherry going to get a shock!

We bowed and I was off the line like a bullet! Mr Sherry was probably expecting a little more respect.

Too late! Bang! I hit him hard and fast, straight in the midriff. It was a corker! I went back to the line, ready to start again.

When Enoeda Sensei awarded me a half-point I had a grin on my face that was so wide you could have parked a car in it! I looked at Sensei Sherry thinking to myself, Yeah, you're gonna get the same again!

But he must have merely turned the engine on the first time. Now he was revved up and ready to go, and he came at me like a rocket! He hit me from one end of the hall – and it's a big hall – to the other. Fists were going in my face, my body, everywhere! I was getting battered. Not only that, but there was a broom cupboard with its door open at the end of the hall and, before I knew where I was, Sensei Sherry had knocked me straight into it! The door swung to behind me and I collapsed in the darkness. My friend Mick Dewey, who was in the class, said that all you could hear were things clattering and clunking as I scrambled around inside.

Sensei Sherry promptly turned round and walked back to the line. I came staggering after him with a bucket on one foot and a mop over my shoulder!

Sensei Sherry had, quite literally, wiped the floor with me, and while I might have covered myself in something that day it certainly wasn't glory. It was great, though, to become a member of such a strong squad and I learned so much from being a part of it.

Chapter 12

A ROOM FULL OF DAVES, A BOX OF CHOCOLATES AND A SAWN-OFF SHOTGUN

I first met Dave Robinson, a man with whom I've had a very close relationship now for over thirty years, in 1971. At the time I didn't know who he was and our first meeting was nearly a real disaster – for me! Here's what happened.

I was working in the barber's and Dave Robinson came in to have his hair cut by Dave Cox. Although I was working on my own client at the time, I couldn't help but notice that Dave R. looked like a really hard bastard. He's over six foot tall and four foot wide. He's not only built like a tank but, as I found out later, he can fight like one, too! Anyway, he took his seat, Dave C. got to work and everything carried on as normal until my girlfriend Sue Long appeared outside.

Sue was a British international swimming champion, and a lovely girl. At that time I was training four or five nights a week and she was training really hard, too, so we'd meet up for lunch and then again at night after we'd finished training. Dave R spotted her in an instant. He said to Dave C., 'Who's the bird on the doorstep?'

Before Dave C. could answer I piped up, 'She's mine.'

To which Dave R. replied, 'Nothing's yours when I'm around, sunshine.'

What I didn't see was Dave R. winking at Dave C., treating all this as a bit of a joke. You have to bear in mind that Dave R. is six years older than I am. At that time he was twenty-five and I was only nineteen. He was a grown man who wasn't taking any of this seriously and I was a lad with a fiery temper, who was suddenly feeling very pissed off.

I made sure that Dave R. got a good look at the razor in my hand, and I whipped the blade round my client's neck really fast – I didn't cut him, mind. Then I looked at Dave R and smiled, just to let him know that I was a hard little bastard!

He didn't say a word. When Dave C. had finished his hair, he just paid his money and left. But he didn't go very far. Actually, he stopped in the doorway with Sue. The next second, he was leaning against the wall chatting to her! What I didn't know was that he was saying, 'Dave tells me you're his girlfriend and I'm just winding him up a bit. So, when you see him looking, smile at me.'

Sure enough, I looked out and saw Sue smiling at him. I went mad! I raced out of the shop like a banshee.

I said to Sue, 'You fuck off home and I'll speak to you later!'

That was not how I normally spoke to her, but I'd lost the plot at that point. I turned to Dave R. and said, 'You, you big fucker, move on! She's not for you!'

Dave R. just smiled broadly and said, 'Oops! Mistake!' I thought, Yeah! And the mistake's all yours!

As I'm sure you're beginning to realise, there are times in my life when I've been completely wrong – and this was one of them!

Dave R. walked off to his car. I watched him go and went back inside. Dave C. had his head in his hands.

He said, 'You fucking idiot! Do you know who that is?'

I said, 'No. And I don't give a fuck!'

He said, 'You will. That's Dave Robinson.'

I had heard of Dave Robinson – everyone had. He had a phenomenal reputation as a hard man and as a top-class DJ as well. So that was Dave Robinson? I didn't show Dave C. one bit of emotion, but inside I went, 'Oh fuck!'

I said, 'What do you reckon he'll do?

Dave said, 'I dunno, but there's no point running 'cos he'll find you. Whatever he does, you'll just have to front it.'

I didn't have long to wait. A few minutes later a bright red mark 10 Jaguar pulled up on the other side of Leyton High Road. The driver pipped the horn just to make sure that we noticed. It was Dave R. He got out of the Jag and walked round to the boot. He was glaring at me all the time and I felt myself getting smaller by the second. I couldn't believe what happened next. Dave R reached into the boot, took out a sawn-off shotgun, loaded it, picked up something else I couldn't see, and strolled casually across the road as if he didn't have a care in the world. I certainly did! I had lots of cares and nowhere to go with any of them!

He walked into the shop and said, 'Right, you little fucker, you've got a choice. You can go round to your girlfriend's and give her these' – he had a box of chocolates in one hand, which was, I realised, the other thing he'd taken out of the boot – 'and tell her that they are from me with love. Or I'll make you a lot shorter than you already are.' He pointed the shotgun at my knees.

It wasn't a hard decision.

I said, 'I'll take the chocolates, if you don't mind.'

He said, 'Good lad. And don't forget – they're with my love.' He gave me the chocolates and walked out.

I took them straight round to Sue and said what I had to. She laughed her head off.

Two weeks later Dave Robinson was back in the shop, asking if my girlfriend had enjoyed her chocolates.

I said, 'Yes, thank you very much.'

He nodded and invited us both to the reopening of a pub that he was deejaying in. It was called the Magnet and Dewdrop on the Isle of Dogs.

We arrived early – I didn't want to keep him waiting – expecting the place to be packed. Instead, it was nearly deserted. Apart from Dave, us two and the barman there were only half a dozen blokes sitting at a table with their sports bags on the floor. I guessed they were footballers having a beer after training.

The pub was small, but beautifully decorated. Dave was working from an elevated stand that was about seven feet higher than the floor. I went up and asked if he wanted a drink.

He said, 'Yeah, I'll have a vodka and tonic, but be ready 'cos it's gonna kick off any minute with those fuckers!' He nodded towards the footballers.

I bought him his vodka, ordered a large one for myself, and sent Sue back to the car. When I went back to the DJ's stand with the drinks, Dave just said, 'When you see me go, steam in!'

He put a record on and the next second he flew off the stand with the tonic bottle in one hand. He hit several of the blokes with it while he was still in the air. A split second later, I was right into them! It was like one of those cartoon scenes of a gang fight where all you see is a big cloud of dust with arms and legs appearing out of it! Within a couple of minutes we've thrown them all out, and their bags after them. The landlord came rushing in to find that his new pub had just lost all of its customers!

I guessed that the fight was the result of some deep-rooted grievance.

I asked Dave, 'What was the agg all about? Some old score you had to settle?'

'No,' he said. 'They were taking the piss out of the records I was playing!'

Chapter 13

'SON, THERE'S A PANDA CAR OUTSIDE.'

Sue Long was my first true love and we were together for a long time. We were both very young, with raging hormones, and all we did was cuddle each other and bonk – which is what you do at that age, I suppose. Apart from our training there was nothing else in the world! Sometimes she'd stay with me in 'the Little House on the Hairy', which is what Dave and me called the flat above the hairdresser's, until three in the morning. There was a dressing table with a big mirror on it in the bedroom, and you could tilt the mirror so you could watch what you were doing. Afterwards I'd escort her home, which was just round the corner, and then walk the three or four miles back to Mum's. I didn't sleep much in those days and I never felt the need to. I don't think Sue did, either.

We had a great time. I was earning very, very good

money, too. I was doing well at the hairdresser's and I was selling bits and pieces that came into the place, such as shirts out of boxes and stuff. Pound for pound, I probably had more money then than I've ever had in my life. So I took Sue everywhere. Anywhere she wanted to go, she went. I used to take her to the London Palladium. We saw Tom Jones, Jack Jones, all the great singers. We went up the West End to have nice meals in top restaurants. I bought her beautiful dresses. It was wonderful.

After a while, we got engaged and decided that it was time to start saving. Instead of going out so much, we used to sit round her house. Her Dad was a nice man. He actually designed the petrol tank for the Harley-Davidson.

I thought everything was going lovely, but, after only two weeks, Sue came in and said, 'I wanna go out.'

I said, 'Hold up, Sue, it's only been two weeks. Let's try to put a bit of money away.'

She shook her head. 'No. I wanna go out!'

Her Dad just raised his eyebrows and said, 'I'm going out to my shed to mess about.'

Which I thought was really nice of him. When he'd gone I said to Sue, 'Give us a break, we're starting to save.'

Sue frowned. 'She said you'd be like this.'

I didn't know what she was talking about. 'Who said what?'

'My sister said that as soon as we get married you'll become just like her husband. We'll never go anywhere. We'll never do anything. It'll change.'

Now her sister was a good-looking girl, but she was very, very jealous of Sue and I knew she wanted to cause us trouble.

I said, 'It's only been two weeks, Sue. We're supposed to be saving up to get married, for fuck's sake.'

Sue wasn't listening. Her sister had really got to her. 'You've got no "go" in you,' she said.

'No "go"?' I said. 'I'll show you fuckin' "go"!'

And I got up and walked out, slamming the door behind me. However, it was a glass-panel door and the glass caved in. I didn't mean it to. I thought, Oh, fuck! and kept on walking.

By the time I'd reached the pavement, Sue was with me, shouting, 'You've broken the door! You've broken the door!'

I said, 'Go away, Sue! Just go away!'

'No! You've broken the door!'

So I pushed her away, and, as I did so, her sister came running at me.

'Keep your hands off my sister!' she screamed, and leaped at me with her arms flying. I picked her up and threw her into a hedge. I didn't hurt her – there wasn't a mark on either of them – but the next minute a man jumped out of a lorry. He said, 'You've just hit those two fucking women!'

I thought to myself, OK! At least I've got a bloke now! Bang!

I knocked him spark out and carried on walking. By now I was starting to feel a bit of regret. After all, Sue's sister had wanted to cause trouble and, because of my temper, she'd succeeded!

A minute later Sue's Dad caught up with me. As I've said, he was a lovely man, a gentleman, not at all violent, but he did spend a lot of time on the firing range. He said, 'You've just hit my daughters!'

I wanted to say to him, 'I haven't hit either of them,' but I was too choked. Now, to be honest, if he'd given me a clump right then, I'd have taken it. But he didn't. Instead, he said, 'I think I'm going to shoot you!'

I told him to fuck off and carried on walking.

A few minutes later a Panda car caught me up. Sue had an uncle who was a copper, so obviously they'd got on to him, hadn't they? The copper got out and said, 'Are you David Hazard?'

'Yes, I am.'

'Right. You'd better get in the car.'

By this point I was very uptight. I said, 'Is that right?' and gave him a clump, too. Then I got in the car and drove it home. Which I thought was fair enough, because he'd wanted me in the car.

When I got home I said to Mum, 'The police are going to come for me in a minute. I've had a do with Sue and it's got a bit ugly.'

As I took my money out of my pockets, Mum went onto the balcony and looked down into the car park. She said, 'Son, there's a Panda car outside. They're here already.'

I said, 'No, Mum. I came home in that.'

The police did arrive later and Mum took me to the door. 'Do you want him?' she asked.

'Yes, he's coming with us.'

Mum pulled up my shirt. 'Have a good look at him,' she said. 'There's not a mark on him and I want him back the same way. If there's a mark on him, I'll come and see you!'

That was it! That was my Mum! In the end, the police just gave me a bit of a lecture and sent me home. The uncle felt fucking embarrassed and the family let it drop. A few weeks later Sue and her family emigrated to New Zealand. It had been on the cards for some time, but the plan had been for Sue to stay with me. That didn't happen. She left when they did and I never saw her again.

Chapter 14

'HE'S THERE AGAIN!'

I passed my first *dan* black belt exam in 1972. I took the grading with four other people who were exceptional and, to be honest, I didn't think I was going to pass. But I was the only one who did! The others all passed on their next attempt, but on that particular day I was on fire – I was buzzing!

I turned up for the next class still wearing my brown belt – I hadn't wanted to tempt fate by buying a black belt before the grading – and Enoeda Sensei walked up to me and said, 'Why are you not wearing a black belt?'

I told him I hadn't got one yet.

He smiled and said, 'Once you are at black belt level you should at least train in your first class wearing a black belt.' With that, he took his belt off and gave it to me! The smile on his face was so wide, and the power that exuded from him was just unbelievable. He took my brown belt, put it on and taught the class wearing that.

I felt amazing! Here I was wearing Sensei's belt! It was like wearing a suit of armour, I felt invincible! The best thing about it was that by swapping belts with me Sensei was making a double statement. He was telling me that I should wear a black belt now and that, no matter what colour belt he was wearing, he was still the Boss. At the end of the class I took his belt off, wrapped it up nicely the way we do in karate, and took it back to him.

'Sensei,' I said, 'here's your belt.'

He shook his head. 'No, now it's yours,' he said. 'I have some others at home.'

And that was it. I had his belt, with his name on it. I'm only five foot seven tall, but when I wore that belt I felt seven foot five!

Even before I passed my first *dan*, I used to follow him all over the place to train. I'd say to him after a class, 'Where are you teaching at the weekend, Sensei?'

He'd just say, 'Busy, busy,' or something like that. He'd never tell me where he was going.

So I had to find out for myself and then I'd just turn up. When he saw me in the class, he'd say, 'Why are you here? This will be the same training as you've been doing all week.'

There was nothing he could say or do, though, to stop me training with him. I just wanted to do karate and be in his environment. There was nothing that mattered more to me. Years later, Reiko, Sensei's wife, told me that he used to come home from a course, throw his bag down and say, 'He's there again! Everywhere I go, he's there!'

Eventually, he accepted the fact that I was going to find out where he was going and one day he said, 'Enough! This weekend I'm going to be in Liverpool.'

I said, 'I know, Sensei.'

He nodded. 'Are you going?'

'Yes, Sensei. I'll see you there.'

'In that case,' he said, 'You may as well come to my house and we will go together.'

I was over the moon! I drove my Singer Chamois (which was the posh version of the Hillman Imp) to his house in Richmond, got out and saw that he'd got a large, 3-litre, mustard-coloured Rover. Things were just getting better! I thought, Wow! I'm going to ride in that car with the Boss of Bosses, train, ride back and then go home. What a day!

When Enoeda Sensei came out, he gave me the car keys and told me to drive. I repositioned the driver's seat and the wing mirrors while he put his bag in the boot. I'm thinking to myself, In a minute, he's going to sit in the front passenger seat and we're going to chat all the way there. It'll be fantastic!

But I was dead wrong. Sensei got in the back seat, took his shoes off and lay down to read a book. We set off. I tried to get a conversation going, but he wasn't having any of it.

'Are you all right, Sensei?'

'Fine. Concentrate on your driving.'

All of a sudden, I looked in the mirror, the book was on his chest and he had nodded off. Now there was no chance of a chat.

I was driving along not paying too much attention to what was happening, when the driver in front of me hit his brakes. I did the same – a bit too hard, to tell you the truth – and Enoeda Sensei was thrown forwards into the well between the seats. He jumped up like a cat and clipped me round the ear.

'What are you doing?'

'It's not my fault Sensei!' I said. 'That fella in front braked too hard.'

'No, you were driving too fast,' Sensei said. 'Also, if you understand distance it doesn't matter how hard the other man brakes.'

I knew better than to argue and we didn't speak again for the rest of the journey. When we arrived Sensei stormed out of the car, took his bag out of the boot and walked off without waiting for me.

Everyone could see that he'd got the hump. Terry O'Neill and all the others were glaring at me, because they guessed it was my fault. In the *dojo*, Sensei did one of his famous very brief warm-ups then told everyone to pair up. I knew what was coming next. He called me out and told me to attack him with a front hand punch to the face. I flew at him. He moved off to the side and hit me in the head with a roundhouse kick.

I saw stars, fell over, and can't remember anything else until I found myself lying on a crash mat at one end of the room. It seems that Terry had picked me up, carried me out of the way and dropped me on the mat. Once I'd come round, I stood up ready to rejoin the class. I must admit I was still feeling groggy, and Enoeda Sensei simply pushed me back down and told me to stay there.

What a great day it had turned out to be! I'd driven from the East End to Richmond, then up to Liverpool, barely spoken to Sensei, managed to send him sprawling in the car, pissed him off, been kicked in the head, missed the entire class and now had to travel back!

In the changing rooms, Sensei said, 'Dabie' (that was

how he always pronounced my name – he couldn't say 'Dave'), 'are you driving?'

'Of course, Sensei,' I said. I've never been one for saying no. Even when my head feels as if it's got bells ringing inside it.

'In that case,' Sensei said, 'don't drive too fast this time.'

'Don't worry about that, Sensei,' I said. 'I won't drive too fast.'

And I didn't. If we were in a thirty mile an hour zone, I drove at twenty eight. If the limit was seventy, I did sixty five. I don't know about driving too fast, but I was definitely driving him to distraction. I didn't care about that. My only concern was making sure he didn't come off that back seat again. (And, perhaps, in making a little point of my own.)

In the end, Sensei couldn't take it any more. He'd had a long day and just wanted to get home.

'Dabie!' He leaned into the front. 'Just hurry up!'

'I'm afraid I can't do that, Sensei,' I said. 'You see, every time I drive too fast I misunderstand the distance between me and car in front, you fall off the back seat and then I seem to get a headache!'

Fortunately, Sensei saw the funny side.

Chapter 15

'JUST DO WHAT YOU NORMALLY DO.'

I made it onto the national team a year after my first squad training and my visit into the broom cupboard. We were fighting at Belle Vue in Manchester against the Belgians. The competition was over two rounds, which meant that you had a go against two of the other team. In my first fight I didn't score a point. It ended in a nil–nil draw. When I sat down Sensei O'Neill told me off.

'What the fuck are you doing?' he asked in his usual blunt manner.

I said, 'I just wanted to win so much.'

He said, 'Look at the fella you've been fighting.'

I did. He looked as if he'd been hit with a bus. I'd caught him with just about everything I'd thrown, but there'd been nothing clinical about my work. It had been raw, rough and ugly.

Sensei O'Neill went on, 'Why do you think you're here?'

I said, 'I dunno.'

He said, 'You were picked because of the way you fight normally. Why were you trying to do more than that? You hit that guy with everything, but you've not scored a point, have you? It was horrible to watch. I've watched you fight for the last year. Just go out and fight like that, just do what you normally do.'

It was great advice. I realised that I'd been trying too hard. In the next round I went out and fought like I normally did. Bang! I scored a full point and sat down with a draw and a win under my belt. Not bad for my first go.

By 1973 karate had been an important part of my life for several years and was becoming increasingly well known and popular throughout the country. Bruce Lee's films were attracting large audiences. Suddenly, it seemed, everyone wanted to be a martial artist. This explosion of interest created a lot of media attention and, one night, Enoeda Sensei came into Blackfriars and said that we were going to do a programme for TV. It was to be part of the *Open Door* series run by the BBC and, as far as we knew, it was the first time a television programme had focused entirely on karate. Sensei picked a team to do the demonstration and told everyone what he wanted of them. It would be a live programme, so there was obviously going to be some pressure.

He said to me, 'You are doing a *kata*, Heian Yondan.'

I thought, Lovely! It's my favourite one.

Then he said, 'And you're doing the *tamashiwari*!'

I wasn't so pleased to hear that. *Tamashiwari* is wood-breaking and at the next class Sensei brought in a block of Japanese hard wood called *obichi*. It was over three inches thick! When he gave it to me I thought he was joking.

'You break this,' he said.

I had broken little bits of wood before, pieces an inch thick, and hurt my hand on those. How was I supposed to break this? I said, 'Sensei, you are kidding, right?'

'No, no, it's easy,' he said. 'I will teach you how to break it.'

I said, 'Better than that, Sensei, why not just do it yourself?'

He laughed, 'No, no, I've got too much to do already. You must break it.'

Sensei was obviously finding this funny, but I wasn't. 'It's so big,' I said.

'Then you must make it small,' he replied.

'What, you mean I can cut it in half?'

He shook his head. 'No. At the moment the wood shocks you, it prevents you from doing what you normally do, so you must take it with you everywhere. You must walk around with it. When you take breakfast, put it on the table. When you go to bed, put it by your pillow. When you go out, take it with you. Everywhere you go I want that bit of wood to go also. Then two things will happen. One, the wood will no longer be so shocking. It will get smaller in your mind. Two, you will become fed up carrying it and you will get so angry that you will want to smash it.'

I did exactly as he told me and, yet again, he was right. After a time the wood didn't seem as shocking.

I took it home and showed Mum and Dad. They said, 'What's that? Why are you walking about with that bit of wood all day long?'

I said, 'I've gotta break it on telly.'

'Get out of it!' they said. 'You can't break that!'

It shocked people everywhere I went. They'd say, 'What are you gonna do with that?'

I'd say, 'I'm gonna bust it on telly.'

'You are joking!'

'Nope.'

And I wasn't. I'd never felt less like joking. You see, no matter what people said, my mind kept making it smaller and smaller. Not only that, I was also getting pissed off having to carry it everywhere!

As we prepared for the programme, I said to Sensei, 'Who do I get to hold the wood for me?'

He said, 'Nobody can hold wood that big. If they try, they will move under the impact and the wood will not break. You must find something that has no give. There is only one place like that – the floor.'

'Oh, right, I see. I'll put two bricks on the floor and put the wood on them?'

Sensei shook his head. 'No, use one brick, not two. Two bricks make it flat, stable. One brick, one edge, finds the biggest weakness.'

I thought that was so clever!

Anyway, the time came round for us to do the programme and everyone did a great job. Kawazoe Sensei and Tomita Sensei did a fantastic demonstration using a large blade. The rest of the team, including Jim Wilson, Ray Kerridge, Tony Harris, Pauline Fuller and me, showed both *kata* and self-defence techniques. The programme was introduced and explained by Bryn Williams, who was the general secretary of the British Karate Control Commission. To be honest, he did a bloody good job, even though he got a bit tongue-tied in places. When he announced the wood breaking it was my moment of truth. I walked out in front of the cameras, put the wood on the floor the way Sensei told me, bottled it a little bit, regained my composure, and then whack! Three inches of Japanese hardwood broke in half. I bowed, picked the bits up, and walked off.

The highlight of the demonstration was, of course, the work done by Enoeda Sensei. He showed his own personal *kata*, took on a group of us, and did loads of basic techniques with Tomita Sensei. It was live telly, going out to the nation, and there he was, proudly representing Japanese karate. He knew everyone was looking and that some people would have been only too pleased if he'd mugged himself off. He knew that he wouldn't get a second chance. Thing is, Enoeda Sensei was the Boss. He didn't need a second chance. He was awesome!

I discovered later that I'd set a record for wood breaking by a European. More importantly, I've got great memories of the night that a programme about Shotokan karate first appeared on the BBC. And I've still got the wood!

Chapter 16

'IF YOU WANT TO FIGHT HIM, YOU'VE GOT TO FIGHT ME FIRST'

There's not much to say about my karate training during this time, other than that I trained like a lunatic, kept following Enoeda Sensei everywhere, and entered a load of competitions to gain experience.

I did win my fair share of titles and, although I don't really want to get into that with you now, I will tell you about one funny competition experience.

I was fighting in the 1976 Karate Union of Great Britain National Championship. The KUGB was the organisation I belonged to. It was – and still is – the largest Shotokan organisation in the country and its national championships, held at Crystal Palace, was a major event with hundreds of competitors and thousands of spectators.

I was fighting well that year and had got through to the semi-finals, where I came up against Vaughan Johnson –

an excellent fighter and a real gentleman. Now, there are two things you need to know about karate competitions in those days, and one thing you need to remember. The first thing you need to know is that fights were won by scoring one point, which you could get for landing two blows worth half a point each, or one 'killing' blow worth a full point. The second thing, however, was that you had to land your blows with a degree of control; if you cut your opponent you were usually disqualified. You also need to remember that there were several thousand people watching me and Vaughan fight.

After a few seconds, we clashed. I went underneath his attack and punched at his stomach. As I did so, his punching arm skidded against my jaw. The referee stopped the fight and gave me a half-point for my stomach punch. I knew straightaway that Vaughan had cut my chin because I felt it go warm. The referee didn't see my injury at first – mainly because I did my best to keep it hidden from him. While I did want to beat Vaughan, I didn't want to win by disqualification. I wanted to outfight him. So, by the time the referee had seen my cut, all he could do was stop the fight, get me patched up and then let us get started again.

As I watched Vaughan move I thought to myself that he was too tall and long-limbed for me to keep off him, so I needed to get in close and kick him. He wouldn't be expecting that.

I have always been able to kick from close in, but this time Vaughan covered my kick beautifully and grabbed me by my crotch and the lapels of my *gi*. Then he picked me up to throw me. Only, as he did so, I grabbed his throat and balls, too. Now we were going nowhere. The entire audience gasped and then fell silent. Everyone, that is, apart from one person. My Mum had come to watch me fight and, as three thousand people held their breath in silence, she shouted out to Vaughan, 'You! Put him down!'

Vaughan did as he was told but, to be honest, it was because the referee had ordered us to stop. I glanced across at Enoeda Sensei, who had a puzzled look on his face, clearly wondering who it was who had shouted out.

'It's my mother,' I said and he nodded briefly, managing to control his smile.

Although I did go on to beat Vaughan, I lost in the final to one of my seniors, Bob Poynton, who is a great *karateka*. Anyway, as I've said, this isn't a book about what I've done and won in competitions. It's a book about the people I've met and the experiences I've had through meeting them, whether they were involved in karate or not. I've always believed that you can learn from everyone – even if what you learn is how not to do something. Everything I am I owe to the influence of other people, especially my family and friends. When I started being successful at karate, friends in the East End were so proud of me that they even did their best to keep me out of fights.

One time I was sitting in the King Harold pub on Leyton High Road enjoying a lemonade with a couple of faces, when this dick came over and said, 'You're that Dave Hazard who does karate.'

I said, 'Yeah, mate. That's right.'

I'd never seen this guy before, but the local paper had run a couple of stories about some of my competition wins and the fact that I'd been picked for the national team.

The guy said, 'I wouldn't mind fighting you if you think you're that clever.'

I was just about to tell him where to go, when one of my friends said, 'Yeah, you can fight him if you want, but he'll knock you scatty. Besides that, you're not gonna fight him. He's just got into the England team and if he knocks you out he'll probably get dropped from it. So, if you want to fight him, you've got to fight me first.'

The guy backed off immediately. He knew my friend could handle himself and he didn't want any of him. He certainly didn't want any of me – he just didn't know that!

There were several other occasions when my friends stopped people from trying to fight me. They valued what I was achieving and didn't want anything or anyone to get in the way of it.

Sometimes, though, friends got me into fights. Often they didn't realise that was what they were doing – they just asked me for help and didn't appreciate how it could all turn out. Sometimes, however, they did it on purpose. My good friend, and senior in Shotokan karate, Terry O'Neill, did his best to get me into a fight after we had competed in the European Championships in Denmark. Fortunately for me, and despite Terry's best efforts, I was able to deal with the problem fairly easily.

It started when we were in a nightclub, having a drink and watching the girls dance. A Danish lump walked up to Terry and said, 'Hello. I do Kyokushinkai karate. I watched the championships today. I don't think Shotokan karate is very good.'

Terry looked at him in his typical, menacing way and said, 'Do you want to fight?'

'Yes,' said the lump. 'I will fight.'

'Right then,' said Terry, pointing at me. 'You see that little fucker over there? Go and have a word with him.'

So the dickhead came over to me. I said to him, 'Let's go outside and sort this out.'

'OK,' he said.

Once we were on the pavement I said to him, 'Look, why don't you show me some of your techniques, then I'll show you what I can do and we'll see if we can resolve this.'

'OK,' he said. 'I will show you.'

And he did a series of punches and kicks, which was just what I wanted. I'd already decided that he deserved a clump, but I thought it made sense to find out what I was up against. He wasn't too bad. He wasn't really good, but he wasn't a doughnut, either.

'Righto,' I said, when he'd finished. 'It's my turn now.'

The guy stood to one side. I took up my fighting stance and prepared to demonstrate my stuff. Only, instead of punching into thin air, I spun quickly in his direction and hit him flush on the chin. He went out like a light.

'See that?' I asked him as he lay unconscious on the pavement. 'That was one of my techniques.'

Unknown to me, Bob Rhodes and Billy Higgins, two other members of the England team and two of my very dear friends, were peering out of the nightclub window watching me, while O'Neill kept his back to them and his eyes on the dance floor.

'Has Hazard done him yet?' Terry asked.

'No,' they said.

'Well, what is he doing?'

'He's just having a chat.'

'What?'

'Now he's watching the other guy do his stuff.'

'What?'

'Oh. It's OK. He's just knocked him out.'

''Bout fucking time.'

Unfortunately, not every conflict I've had has been as easy to manage as that one. A far more serious situation occurred at a party I went to with Dave Robinson and his brothers, Chris and Harry.

Dave was working at a pub called the Black Boy in Bethnal Green at the time. He was the DJ there, but he also made sure that no one kicked off. Anyway, we got invited to a party organised by a tidy little crew who called themselves 'Rent a Crowd'. We accepted the invitation and went along.

The party was going well, when Harry had a verbal pop at someone. Chris heard him and said, 'You're out of order. We're guests of these people, so shut the fuck up!'

All three brothers started arguing and, the next thing I knew, they'd gone outside for a fight!

I went out after them. Sure enough, Dave and Harry were squaring up to each other.

Chris said to me, 'Stop them from having a go.'

I said, 'Fuck me! They're your brothers!'

He said, 'Yeah, but they'll listen to you.'

So I got in between the pair of them and got them apart. Chris then decided that the best thing to do was go back inside and apologise on behalf of his brother. In he went. A minute later, he came staggering out with claret on his face. The door slammed behind him.

He said, 'They jumped me!'

Dave looked at me and said, 'Hazard, open that door.'

As I moved towards it, Dave went in the opposite direction. I knew that he was going to his car boot and that there wouldn't be any chocolates in it this time.

I kicked the door open and rushed inside. There was a glass door to my left. I saw a guy on the other side of it and punched straight through the glass, knocking him out and cutting my hand in the process. Behind me, Harry had pulled the phone off the wall so that he could hit people with it. As I ran into the main room a couple of guys came at me. I punched the first one, then grabbed the other, kneed him in the stomach and threw him to one side. His head went through the TV screen. It wasn't what I meant to do and it was unfortunate, but, that said, it was the only way he was ever going to get on the box!

Harry was in another room and I saw him clump someone with the phone and punch someone else. I heard all this squealing and screaming coming from the kitchen and saw a load of girls jumping out of the window. It was pandemonium. There was blood flowing, people shouting and girls flashing their knickers as they jumped for safety. The next thing I heard was Dave Robbo shout, 'Everybody down!'

And then he fired his shotgun in the air.

Everyone dived for cover and we got out of there. Which was just as well, since there were forty to fifty blokes at the party and the four of us would have got murdered!

We knew the police would turn up and start looking for everyone who'd been involved, so we drove to a hospital that was out of the way. We were also hoping that the guys we'd clumped would use the local hospital.

We were proved to be half right. The police did arrive quickly, but by then most people had gone – including the guys we'd bashed. Unfortunately, they'd decided to use the same hospital we had.

Chris and I were being looked after in Casualty. There was a nurse doing a good job of stitching my hand up when, behind me, a guy came in on a stretcher. He had his brother beside him. The guy on the stretcher pointed at me and said, 'That's him! That's the one who did it to me.'

His brother did no more than pick up a chair, come over, and hit me on the head with it! The nurse fell off her chair, screaming, and there I was with a needle in my finger, cotton hanging down from it, and a bloody great cut in my head. A scuffle broke out and we left the hospital in a hurry.

When I thought about it, I couldn't believe what had happened. I'd gone out for a good time at a party, had to stop two brothers fighting, kicked a door open, cut my hand punching through glass, clumped a few people, been bashed over the head with a chair, and left hospital with more injuries than I had when I went in!

A few days later a fella walked into the Black Boy and put a gun to Dave's head. He wanted to know where to find me. Dave told him to fuck off.

The man said, 'I'll give you a few days to think about it.' He put his gun away and turned to leave.

Dave said, 'Oi! When you pull a gun on someone you should use it. You know that, don't you?'

At which point he promptly administered his own unique form of comeuppance!

He then phoned me and told me what had happened.

le as a young lad.

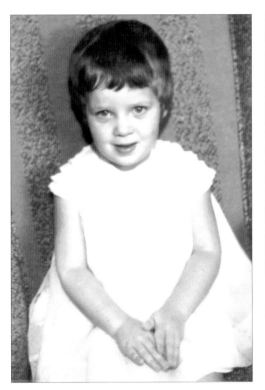

Above left: Our little angel, Janice.

Above right: The Little Princess, Tracey.

Below: My Mum and Ben on their wedding day. My beloved Nan is just behind my Mum's shoulder on the left.

My mentor and great friend, Dave Cox.

Me and Deborah on our wedding day on 23rd September 1982 (*above*). My close friend of over thirty years, Dave Robinson and his lovely wife Tracy on their wedding day (*below*).

Above: Karen at our favourite restaurant in Hove, East Sussex 1988.

Left: My great friend Richard La Plante.

Above: The very best of muckers … Mick Dewey and me.

Below: The old boys out on the town enjoying the 'Bib Course' in Nottingham. Left to right: Billy Higgins, Bob Rhodes, me and Mick Dewey.

ove: Janice, Mum, Tracey, Ben and me at Ben's 80th birthday party.

low: Tracey and Mum now.

Above left: Ben the Man and Mum on holiday.

Above right: A beautiful and classy lady with a heart of gold, my sister Janice.

Below: The beautiful Paula with me on holiday.

'For what I've just done for you,' Dave said, 'you owe me a half of lager.'

I laughed. 'Shouldn't it be a pint?'

'No,' he said. 'He wasn't worth a pint.'

Chapter 17

WHIZZBANG!

I worked for a time with my Uncle John, who was the husband of my Mum's eldest sister. He was an auto electrician. I loved working with him because I've always had a thing for cars and, more importantly, Uncle John was the kindest, gentlest and most helpful man you could ever wish to meet. He's passed away now, but he had a fantastic reputation and I loved him to bits.

Anyway, this whizzbang – a cocky, young lad – came in one day. He had a nice car, a continental, a make that was always hard to work on, and he left it with us. Uncle John spent a lot of hours on the car and, by the time he was done, the bill came to over a hundred quid – which was a lot of money in those days.

The whizzbang returned, collected his car and drove off, promising to pay in the next few days. I had a nasty feeling that we wouldn't see him again, but Uncle John was far more trusting than me. Sad to say, the whizzbang didn't let me down. He just disappeared, thinking, perhaps, that I was the sort of person who'd forget about it.

A couple of weeks later, Johnny Farley phoned me to say that I needed to go to the hospital because Chris Robinson was there. It seemed that he'd been in a fight that had gone wrong and was in a bad way. Chris and me used to work the doors together and this particular night he'd been there without me. So off I went, not knowing what to expect.

When I saw him I was really shocked. I couldn't recognise him! He'd taken such a hiding that his face was really disfigured. I asked what had happened and was told that Chris had made the fatal error of throwing a couple of guys out of the pub and then followed them out. For a doorman, there are a whole host of reasons why you don't want to find yourself fighting out on the street, but on this occasion Chris had got himself there. Unfortunately for him, one of the guys was obviously well trained – he was a boxer, I think – and he'd done Chris big time. If someone had shown me a photo of Chris's face, I wouldn't have known who it was!

'Don't worry,' I said to him. 'I'll get you out of here as soon as you're ready.'

The doctors did all the necessary checks and found, thankfully, that there was no permanent damage. A day or two later, when they said he could go, I picked him up as promised.

As I was driving him home, towards Stratford, who should I see going in the opposite direction but the whizzbang in his continental! I said to Chris, 'Sorry, mate. I've got to follow this bloke. He's turned my uncle over.'

I spun the car round and set off after him, flying down the road with the Elephant Man sitting next to me.

I could see that the whizzbang had a couple of mates in his car, which meant that it was going to be me against the three of them, because Chris was in no fit state to scrap. Then, as luck would have it, I saw Johnny Farley driving the other way. I flashed him and he turned round and followed me.

Eventually the whizzbang pulled up. I stopped right behind him, leaped out of my car and began explaining to him that he needed to pay my uncle immediately. His mates showed no desire to get involved, which I put down to the fact that I was clearly not happy and that Johnny was standing next to me with a crowbar in his hand. The whizzbang promised to pay what he owed, so I let him go. When I turned round there was Chris Robbo, standing behind me with his fists raised, peering out of the two tiny slits that were his eyes.

'We'll have 'em, Dave,' he said.

I said, 'Fuck me, Chris. Get back in the car. You'll scare people to death looking like that.'

I'm sure that, if someone had just touched his face, Chris would have been in unbearable agony but, credit where credit is due, he was there, ready to have a go. He wasn't thinking about the possible consequences.

The whizzbang paid his debt the next day. Uncle John, bless him, saw it as another example of the honesty and good nature of all people.

'I told you he could be trusted, Dave, ' he said to me. 'I told you he could.'

Chapter 18

CONSEQUENCE

*I*n truth I have never thought too much when it has kicked off. I just get on with it. I let my training and my instinct and the adrenaline deal with it. It's only afterwards that I analyse what happened in the conflict. I think about what they did and how I reacted. Then I do a bit of research if possible. I find out who they are. Was it just a mug, or someone who is connected?

I learned early on that, in conflict, you don't have time to think. The thought processes take too long. You can't think, 'Will I do this, then that?' You don't have that much time – and the way I fight you certainly don't.

What stops most people is the thought of consequence. 'What if I lose?' 'What if I win and he comes after me?' 'What if I win and the police arrest me? Will I lose my job? Will I go to prison?' And, worst of all, 'Will he come after my family?' All these thoughts can fuck you up.

Fuck losing! Fuck the police, the job – even fuck my family! I'm no good to my family if I'm the one laying on the ground, bleeding.

In my view, you deal with consequences after. There might be none. There might be a lot. But at least you are up and running and, after they've had a good hiding, they might think twice about a come-back. Especially if they know you don't give a fuck.

Chapter 19

UNDERNEATH
THE ARCHES

One day Sensei asked me to go to the airport to pick up a new Japanese assistant instructor. It was Tomita Sensei. He arrived at the airport, very quiet, looking as hard as nails and as fit as fuck. He was obviously fresh from the JKA instructors' course. I found out later that he'd just won the Japan Universities Championships. I must say, at that time his technique wasn't brilliant but, boy, could he fight and train hard!

Enoeda Sensei had realised that he needed an assistant, so he'd gone back to Japan to look at the new influx into the instructors' class. He'd seen Tomita Sensei, liked him, and persuaded him to come to England. The plan was that Sensei would complete his training as an instructor and, in return, Tomita would assist with the teaching. It wasn't long before Enoeda Sensei had transformed Tomita into a brilliant *karateka*. Wherever he went, he was highly regarded and loved. He had a lovely balance about him. He was a great technician, fighter and teacher.

I remember a night at Blackfriars when Tomita Sensei was teaching the beginners – I'd just got my black belt by this time – and we had a very minor problem with one of the many tramps who spent the nights under Blackfriars bridge.

There are loads of little arches under the bridge and the drunk, homeless people would spend the night tucked up inside them. Sometimes they'd wander over to the hall to see what all the noise was about. Some were just curious, others were keen to fight. After all, even a fight in the warmth was better than what they were used to. Once in a while a really nasty piece of work would stagger into the *dojo*, and I'll tell you about one of those in a minute. This particular night, though, a group of us were waiting in the foyer for the beginners' class to finish when, all of a sudden, the door opened and in walked a drunk. He tried to go through into the *dojo*.

I stopped him, 'Not tonight, mate,' I said. 'We're busy.'

He immediately started to make a fuss. I was just about to make him leave when one of the purple and white belts, a nice guy called Kevin Murphy, suddenly got in my way saying, 'Dave! You can't do anything to him, you're a black belt now. You're one of the seniors. I'll deal with him instead.'

At which point Kevin slapped him gently round the face and tried to turn him round. The guy wasn't having any of it. He started reaching into his jacket pocket, saying, 'I'll stab you! You fuck!'

Kevin shouted, 'Dave! He's got a knife!'

I spun round, expecting the worst and ready for anything. However, to be fair, the guy still managed to surprise me. He was holding the tiniest penknife that I'd ever seen. And he'd still got it folded shut! He was trying desperately to open it, but his hands were shaking so much from the drink, and his eyesight was obviously so bad that he just couldn't manage it. I couldn't bring myself to hit him properly – he didn't need it – so I jabbed him in the face just hard enough to make him stagger backwards. He went out of the door, still fumbling with his penknife, and fell over a bench.

Tomita Sensei had heard the noise and came running out, asking what had happened. I didn't really want to tell him that I'd just clumped someone at the *dojo* door, in case he gave me a good hiding. On the other hand, the tramp was still lying on the ground. How was I going to explain that away?

Before I could speak, Kevin came to my rescue, saying, 'Sensei! Sensei! The man had a knife!'

Tomita Sensei said to me, 'Is it true?' Then, just as I was about to explain that it was only a little penknife, he went on, 'If he had a knife, how did you hit him?'

I said that I'd jabbed him in the face. Tomita shook his head, saying that, because the man had a knife, I should have kicked him.

'Go! Kick him now!' he ordered.

I couldn't refuse and gave him the most gentle kick I could possibly do while pretending to kick him really hard. Poor old boy, I thought, that could be me in a few years.

The other drunk I'm going to tell you about was a different kettle of fish altogether. He was a nasty, violent drunk who wanted to hurt someone, a right bastard, who pushed his way into the *dojo* one night when I was teaching a class. As I went towards him he immediately shaped up to hit me, so I let him have it. Then I dragged him to one side and put him in a corner. Please understand, this was a dangerous man and I was concerned that, if I'd just thrown him out, he'd have attacked the first person he ran into. So I waited to see what mindset he was in when he woke up.

Anyway, it wasn't long before he came round. He started screaming, making it clear that he still wanted to fight, so, while the class was working, I popped over and gave him another one. He was asleep a bit longer this time. The next time he came round he did the same thing again, challenging everyone in the room. The students had their backs to him and I said to Terry Eden, the former ABA champion, 'Do you want a pop?'

He nodded, charged over and knocked the guy out again. The bloke woke up again a few minutes later, but this time he'd sussed what would happen if he tried to be violent. He half-sat up, saw me looking at him and slumped down again. I knew what his game was. He played possum until the class ended. Then I ordered all the students into the kitchen, which doubled as our changing room. From there, I watched as the man peeped first out of one eye, then out of the other. Once he was sure we'd gone, he jumped to his feet and raced out of the door.

I think it would have been far better for him that night if he'd stayed underneath the arches.

Chapter 20

A BRIDGE TOO FAR

One of the nicest memories I've got of Tomita Sensei is when his wife, Turumi, came over to England. He brought her to the *dojo*, even though she couldn't have been long off the plane. In he came, walking very proud, while she tiptoed behind him. He introduced her to me, and she sat down to watch him teach. It was a great class.

Afterwards he walked out of the *dojo*, carrying his bag, hardly giving her a glance as he passed. She just got up and followed him. What neither of them knew was that Dave Cox and me left the *dojo* just after them and we watched as Tomita Sensei marched along while Turumi followed in silence. By the time they were crossing the bridge, she was still behind him. Then he glanced over his shoulder to make sure that none of us were around – fortunately, he didn't see us – and his hand just reached out behind him. Turumi shot forwards instantly, her hand slipping into his. On they went, side by side, their hands swinging as they walked. What a lovely, lovely sight!

Another memory I have of Tomita Sensei also involves a bridge, but in a different way. A team of foreign *karateka* visited the Marshall Street Shotokan Karate Centre during a lunchtime class and told Tomita Sensei that they'd come to fight Sensei Enoeda's team. What did this have to do with a bridge? Easy. By the end of the day the cheeky fuckers realised that when they challenged us they'd gone a bridge too far.

When they issued their challenge to Tomita Sensei, he didn't bat an eyelid. 'Fine,' he said. 'Come back tonight.' Once they'd gone, he phoned me and said, 'Dave, get me a team ready, please.'

I immediately phoned Bob Waterhouse, Dave Vaughan and a few other faces who could all kick off. By the time we arrived at the *dojo* that night, we were all up and ready!

You see, our challengers hadn't gone about this in a polite and respectful way, and we intended to make that clear to them. Assuming that they understood *dojo* etiquette, they had chosen to ignore it in order to force us to have a scrap. If they didn't know how to behave, well, then, they should have done their homework first, because now we were going to teach them a hard lesson. One way or another, they were going to get it!

Both teams lined up. I got up first and so did their top guy. Tomita Sensei, who was refereeing, called us together. We bowed and then started fighting. I let him have it big time! By the time Tomita Sensei told me to stop, their guy was in a heap on the floor with a fair bit of claret all over the place. His team all leaped to their feet, wanting to protest about the rough treatment he'd received. My lot were up immediately, thinking that it was going to kick off big time. Tomita Sensei was in between us in a flash, ordering us to sit down. We, of course, did as we were told. We sat and stared at our visitors, all of whom had clearly planned to come to our *dojo* and give us a kicking. But their plan had backfired.

Tomita Sensei said to them, 'You! Pick him up!' He gestured towards the guy on the floor. 'And then all of you go! Next time you visit a *dojo*, show respect!'

As I've said, Tomita Sensei was a man who showed respect and received it from all who knew him. He did a lovely thing for me the day I left England to train in Japan. He actually came to the airport to see me off! I was really surprised to see him there and asked him where he was going. 'Home,' he said.

'Where have you been?'

'Nowhere.'

'Oh.' Now I was confused.

'I've come to say goodbye.' Now I was shocked.

He said, 'I remember you came to the airport to meet me when I first arrived in England, so now I am doing the same for you.'

He gave me a card, signed by both him and Turumi, in which he'd written, 'Go your way for the great *kiai*!' He'd also put a ten-thousand-yen note in the card. I didn't understand Japanese money then and decided I was probably rich. Fuck me! I thought. I bet I can buy Japan with this!

The truth was it was just enough to buy a meal. The more important truth is, that it was a lovely gesture from a true gentleman.

Chapter 21

'HOW DID YOU EVER GET KNOCKED ON YOUR ARSE WITH FEET THAT BIG, MR COOPER?'

Enoeda Sensei arranged for us to do a demonstration at the Café Royal as part of a retirement party for a sports writer, Donald Zegg. It was going to be quite a big event. Top of the bill was Henry Cooper, the boxing legend, who was going to spar with his brother. We were next up, led by Tomita Sensei. After that there was going to be a wrestling demonstration by the great Mike Marino, followed by Dave Prowse, who was going to do some bodybuilding. Prowse went on to become famous, first as the Green Cross Man and then, on the big screen, as Darth Vader in *Star Wars*.

We arrived on the night to find that Henry Cooper's brother couldn't come and that Henry had cancelled the boxing. If you think about it, you couldn't blame him. We'd agreed to do a demo because we had a team of people who all knew what they were doing – remember, it was an evening of demonstrations, not fights – and we wouldn't have performed with people we didn't know and trust. It was exactly the same for Mr Cooper. Even more so in some ways, because he was a legend with absolutely nothing to prove. So, with the boxing sidelined, we became top of the bill.

While we were all backstage warming up, stretching and stuff, Dave Prowse made a comment, taking the piss out of what we were doing. Quick as a flash, I made a comment back. Prowse stiffened and straightened up. He was clearly happy to make what he thought were clever comments, but not happy to have something come back in his direction. Now, Dave Prowse is a tall guy and, as you know, I'm not. Still, as he straightened, I went whoosh! and put a roundhouse kick right up by his face. It was perfectly controlled, so it didn't do him any damage.

He still didn't like it, though, and he snarled, 'I'll snap you in half, you little fuck!'

I said, 'Whenever you like.'

Before Prowse could move, Mike Marino said to him, 'Leave the kid alone or you'll have me to deal with.'

Prowse stopped dead in his tracks. Any thoughts he had of treating me like a twiglet disappeared from his mind – not because of me, but because of Mr Marino. Christ, he was good! I've always had respect for really good wrestlers. If they get their hands on you you're in real trouble, they can break you into bits, and Mr Marino wasn't just a good wrestler – he was a great wrestler!

After our demo, we sat watching the rest of the boxing show when Henry Cooper joined us. He said, 'I wish I'd known some of that karate stuff when I was boxing.'

We all laughed. I looked down and saw that he'd got huge feet. I said, 'Fuck me! How did you ever get knocked on your arse with feet that big, Mr Cooper?'

He just looked at me and said, 'In a minute one of these is going right up your arse!'

For once I knew better than to come back with a smart reply. I just said, 'Fair enough,' and changed the subject.

I was a young kid who spoke before he thought. Mr Cooper was a class act. He had no edge to him whatsoever. It was a privilege to have spent some time with him, and to have watched Mr Marino work.

Chapter 22

'GET AT 'EM!'

While I was training at Blackfriars, I was asked to look after a pub which, funnily enough, was just around the corner from the *dojo*. It had been taken over by a guy I knew called Wooper. He was called that because he went 'Woop!', which was an East End greeting, whenever he met you. He asked me if I'd look after his pub while he was out for the night. What he didn't tell me was that he'd fallen out with a south London gang and was worried about the possibility of trouble. Anyway, I said, 'All right,' and went to the pub after training. I just sat at the end of the bar and minded my own business. Everyone behaved themselves and, at the end of the night, I stayed behind to have a little drink and a chat with Wooper's wife, Christine, and the barman.

All of a sudden, bang! – and all the windows came

through. There were bricks being thrown in, gunshots going off and Wooper's Alsatian dog yelping his head off because the glass had cut him. I leaped on top of Christine to shield her and the barman dropped to the floor. Fortunately, the people outside didn't come in, they just shot the pub to bits. My immediate instinct when the shooting stopped was 'Get at 'em!'

I grabbed the barman and said, 'Are you up for this?'

He said, 'Yeah!' and picked up a piece of wood from behind the bar.

We ran outside and saw them legging it towards a Transit van. We jumped into my car and got after them. As we got closer, I saw the gun still in the hands of one of them and thought, Whoa!

I said to the barman, 'I don't fancy getting out with that there, do you?'

Not surprisingly, he didn't, either, although I think he reckoned that we were going to turn round and go back to the pub. No way! I didn't fancy getting out of the car, but I still wanted to have 'em! A gun is a very dangerous weapon, but so is a car. Three of the gang realised that when I ran them over!

Then we raced back to the pub. I told the barman to get Christine out of the building and somewhere safe. I drove my car to a lockup that I had and parked it there. Apparently, the barman had had more than enough. It seems he ignored Christine, packed his bags and was never seen again. When I got home, I had to explain to Ben that he wouldn't be able to borrow my car for a couple of days. 'Sorry, Dad,' I said, 'but I've had a bit of a bang in it.'

Wooper denied ever knowing that it was going to

happen, but by then it was out of his hands anyway. I knew it wasn't going to take these people long to find out who I was, where I was, and then come looking. So, thinking there was a high probability of a comeback, I arranged for myself, Robbo and a good guy called Dave Saunders to go back to the pub. We made sure that lots of people knew we were going to be there.

Dave R. and Dave S. were both tooled up and sat at the end of the bar with their little bags. A fella came in. He was really bashed up. He saw us sitting there and came straight over.

He said simply, 'We want to let it go from here.'

I said, 'Fair enough, but we're also ready to go the other way if you want to.'

He shook his head, said, 'No,' and left.

We never heard from them again.

I don't think Wooper had the pub for very long after that.

Chapter 23

'HELLO. I'M DAVE HAZARD FROM ROUND THE CORNER'

Blackfriars *dojo* closed because they wanted to use the hall as a place for mentally handicapped kids. From the time I'd started there to the time it closed I'd gone from the most basic beginner to running it, which was a weird feeling. Actually, it seemed incredible given that I'd originally wanted only to get a yellow belt.

Blackfriars was a special *dojo*. I met and worked with some very special people there. It was, though, only the first of many great *dojos* that I trained in. When Blackfriars closed, Enoeda Sensei set up two new ones. They were the Shotokan Karate Centre at Philbeach Gardens and what was to become the world-famous Marshall Street Shotokan Karate Centre in Soho. He taught at Philbeach Gardens sometimes, but I ran that mostly. I trained at Marshall Street most days of the week. Some of the students from Blackfriars went there, too, while some went their own way. Marshall Street became home to some great *karateka*, including Jim Wilson, Hugh Achilles, Ian Cheek and Ray Kerridge. The training at Marshall Street was technically outstanding, extremely intense and, at times, ferocious. Which is no surprise when you think that it was Enoeda Sensei's *dojo* and he had Tomita Sensei assisting.

One time, I arrived at the *dojo* and saw that I was the senior grade present. Now, the *dojo* was a big, long room – miles long – and I was warming up right down at the end, waiting for Enoeda Sensei to come in and start the class, when in walked this tall, wiry, bespectacled black belt whom I'd never seen before.

He shook hands with everyone, and I could hear him saying, 'Good evening. I'm Stan Schmidt, South Africa.'

When he reached me, he said the same thing. I replied, 'Hello. I'm Dave Hazard from round the corner.'

He said, 'Oh. I see.'

Then Sensei walked in. Everyone lined up immediately, and this cheeky South African bastard got in front of me to start the class. What you have to understand is, in a karate class the senior grade starts the class – you can actually tell the students' seniority by where they stand in the line-up – and this cheeky bastard had taken my place! I looked at him and thought, You're mine. I'm having you!

Sensei warmed up the class and I was stretching, looking at the back of this bloke's head, thinking, You saucy bastard! You're really gonna get it!

We did some basics, then Sensei said, 'Pair up!'

Schmidt turned round and I was in his face like a shot, making sure that no one else got to him before me. Now, do you remember the mistake I made when I first met Dave Robinson, when I didn't care who the guy was in front of me and was too up for it for my own good? Well, this was just about to turn into another one of those situations, but without the roomful of Daves, the box of chocolates or the shotgun.

Sensei told us to do *jiyu-ippon*, a sparring drill in which each partner attacks in turn with several predetermined punches and kicks. The attacker says what he's going to do and then really goes for it. The defender has to block the attack and control his counter because it is a free shot – the attacker is not allowed to move away or defend. Schmidt was going to attack me first. I planned to counter him with control and yet with enough force to make sure he knew I was there. He told me, in Japanese, the punch he was going to do.

'*Jodan!*' which means 'face punch'. I was more than ready for whatever he'd got to offer. The next second, bang! He hit me right in the face. I didn't even see it!

I thought, You lucky bastard!

I prepared for his next attack. He hit me so hard in the stomach that I thought, Hold up! This isn't luck! This fella's really good! You'd better wake up, Hazard, 'cos he's coming at you next with those long legs!

I woke up. If I'd wanted him before, I really wanted him now. It didn't make any difference. The next minute, whoosh! – he kicked me right up against the wall.

When it was my turn to attack, I went at him like a train. That didn't make any difference, either. He just pushed me away and then battered me! It didn't matter what I did, he just treated me like a baby.

When we'd finished, I looked round and Sensei was

pissing himself! He stopped the class and said, 'I'd like to introduce you to Stan Schmidt, fifth *dan*, Chief Instructor for South Africa.'

Of course, Enoeda Sensei had known how I would react to this newcomer, and had enjoyed watching me learn some painful lessons.

After the class, Schmidt Sensei came up to me and said, 'Very good spirit, young man. Very good.'

I thanked him. What else could I do? I'd just tried to take out the most senior Western Shotokan *karateka* on the planet! What a doughnut!

What I didn't realise was that Schmidt Sensei was over for the course at Crystal Palace. Every year we'd get a few South Africans there and quite a few of them had a bit of an edge to them. Schmidt Sensei wasn't like that, though.

When I got to the course, Schmidt Sensei was there with some of his group, and so was my old mate Mick Dewey. As we've always shared things, I thought I'd share my experience of Schmidt Sensei with Mick. He asked me if there was anyone he needed to watch out for. I pointed to Schmidt Sensei and said, 'You see that lanky fucker over there? He's one of those leery South Africans. I'd give him a dig first chance you get. Don't let him take any liberties.'

When we paired up to scrap I saw Mick go straight for Schmidt Sensei, so I said to the fella I was with, 'Listen, let's not get too excited here. Let's just watch the two over there. It should be fun.'

Now, Mick has the heart of a lion. He doesn't know backwards – I'm sure even his car doesn't have reverse – so I knew he was really going to go after Schmidt Sensei. Sure enough, the pair of them bowed, Mick attacked and, a split second later, went flying up in the air. He leaped to his feet and had another go, with exactly the same result. Mick is a big bloke and, as I watched him flying all over the place, I didn't feel so bad about what had happened to me at the hands and feet of Schmidt Sensei.

At the end of the class Mick came over to me and said, 'Who the fuck is that?'

I said, 'That's Stan Schmidt Sensei. Good, isn't he?'

Mick realised I'd set him up. He groaned and pulled a face. 'Thanks, mate,'

I grinned. 'Come on, Mick,' I said. 'What are mates for?'

Chapter 24

STEEL FIXING

Apart from everything else that was going on I enjoyed a variety of jobs, too. I'd stopped hairdressing so that I could concentrate more on training, and I took lots of little jobs to get different experiences and to earn the money I needed to keep me going. For a time I worked as a steel fixer.

I knew nothing about steel fixing. I'd met some guys in a pub who told me about the job and promised to give me a few tips. Steel fixers are not the same as steel erectors, who work high up, putting girders in place. Steel fixers start out at ground level, making the frames that go in the shuttering so that when concrete is poured in it is reinforced with steel. As a fixer you make your way up the building as it grows. That's why you don't notice the height. You can end up working eleven or more floors up, but you don't think about it because you've gone up bit by bit.

While I was working on this site I was asked to find out if the crane driver was willing to do a bit of extra lifting. I didn't know at the time precisely what the extra lifting would involve and, since I owed a favour to the person who asked, I agreed to have a quiet word. Sure enough, the crane driver was available as long as the price was right. I put him in touch with my colleague and forgot about the whole thing. A week later my colleague was in touch again.

'The crane driver let me down,' he said. 'It's cost me money and loss of face.'

I found out that there had been a plan to remove the steel from the site by using the crane to lift it into a waiting lorry. The steel was worth quite a lot of money, and my colleague had agreed a deal with a potential buyer. He had also paid for the lorry as well as for a number of helpers. At the last minute the crane driver had suffered a change of heart and had refused to go through with it.

'I need him to understand that he owes me for the money I've spent,' my colleague said. 'Would you have a word with him?'

As luck would have it, I had arranged to have a drink that night with Chris Robinson in the pub where most of the building site guys went after work. I promised my colleague that if the crane driver was there I'd explain the problem and encourage him to pay up.

When I met Chris outside the pub I told him that I'd got to have a private word with a fella about a bit of business. Chris spotted that I wasn't too happy.

'Has someone let you down?' he asked.

'Something like that,' I said. 'But all I really have to do

is pass on a message. If the guy's sensible, he'll just wipe his mouth and do the right thing.'

Chris chuckled. 'And if he isn't sensible are you going to give him one of those karate kicks in the head?'

'No,' I said. 'Besides, we don't do things like that – not wearing jeans and boots. That high-kicking stuff is just for the films.'

I walked into the pub, saw the crane driver and had a quiet word. He didn't want to know. I tried to make it clear to him that he'd upset some serious people and didn't have a choice. He glared at me. I knew then that he'd made the mistake of confusing the message with the messenger.

'Perhaps we should talk about this outside,' he snarled.

I said, 'Yeah! Right!'

I turned to walk to the door and he followed me. To my mind this guy had no reason to get pissed off with me. All I'd done was ask him a question in the first place and share some information in the second. Now he wanted to give me a clump! No, he didn't! Hold up! He wanted to do more than that. As I glanced over my shoulder I saw him pick up a Guinness bottle and hide it behind his back.

I thought, Right! Now you're really gonna get it!

As soon as we were outside, the driver pointed the bottle at my face, told me what he was going to do to me with it, and turned to smash it against the wall. I don't know if you are aware of this, but a Guinness bottle is really hard. The guy swung it against the wall, didn't watch what happened, and turned back to threaten me with what he thought would be a jagged half-bottle. Unfortunately for him, the bottle hadn't broken. It took him a second to realise that and, when he did, his mouth dropped open in disbelief. Which is exactly when I kicked him flush in the jaw. Crash!

The driver collapsed, the bottle falling from his hand. The driver's jaw was badly broken, but the bottle didn't even smash when it hit the pavement. It was clearly tougher than he was!

When I turned round to look at Chris Robinson, he was chuckling again. 'Good job those high kicks are just for the films,' he said.

Funnily enough, the same crane driver had played a part in what could have been my ultimate downfall a couple of months earlier. I was working a fair way up at the time, ten or eleven storeys, when his crane lifted a couple of tons of steel and swung it into position just behind me. I stopped what I was doing and began directing him using hand signals. The driver followed my lead and lowered this massive weight down. It was about ten feet away from me when it started moving slowly in my direction. Here's the strange – and very stupid – thing: it was going so slowly that I thought I could stop it by just putting my hand up! There was nothing behind me but thin air, a ninety-foot drop and certain death, and there I was trying to stop two tons of steel with my palm! When it hit my hand it felt like a brick wall – but a brick wall that was moving towards me.

The ganger saw that I was about to get knocked over the edge and shouted, 'Get down, you prick!'

His urgency brought me to my senses and I dropped flat. The steel swung gently over me, out beyond the building and then back again. If I'd stayed on my feet for half a second longer I'd have ended up on the ground looking like a squashed tomato!

Chapter 25

'HEATHCLIFF, IT'S ME...
COME HOME!'

Tony Jarvis was a senior of mine at Blackfriars. He was a fantastic *karateka*, very intelligent and very thoughtful. His brother, Mick, was one of the people I came up through the ranks with. Tony taught a class at Goldsmiths College and he invited me down to help him. One of the black belts at Goldsmiths was a guy called Dr John Bush – remember that name, because I'll come back to him in a bit. Another member of the club was a Peruvian, a brown belt, who, for talking's sake, we'll call Dayo.

Dayo invited Tony to Peru to introduce Shotokan karate over there. Dayo explained that there were no instructors in the country and that interest would be high. It seemed that it might be a good idea, and Tony spoke to Enoeda Sensei about it. At that time Tony was getting ready to take his second *dan* grading. Sensei told him that he could go if he wanted to, but advised him to wait until he had passed the grading. Tony took Sensei's advice – most people did most of the time – and travelled out to Peru as a second *dan*. Once he was there, he discovered that there was a Japanese instructor already living there and that karate was well known. Not to put too fine a point on it, Tony quickly found himself in a bit of a mess. At which point Dayo and his family turned their backs on him. Tony's difficulties increased and, in the end, things got so bad that he had to jump on a merchant ship and work his passage home.

It had clearly been a distressing time for Tony and, when he told me the story, I found it upsetting too. Fortunately, though, I've got a very good memory. It tends to work even better when someone's caused trouble for my family or friends. When I say 'fortunately', I mean fortunately for Tony and me. It turned out to be very unfortunate for Dayo...

In 1975 I was picked to go to Los Angeles as part of the English squad at the JKA World Championships. All the fighters were at a reception before the tournament started, when who should walk in but the Peruvian team, including my good mate Dayo! I recognised the prick instantly. He recognised me, too, and came towards me, putting his hand out as if we were mates or something. No chance! I felt like knocking him out right there and then.

I told him, 'Fuck off! You got Tony into a lot of shit and it's not something I'll ever forget.'

Meanwhile some of my teammates are saying to me, 'What are you doing? Remember where you are. Master Nakayama's standing over there.'

Master Nakayama was the Chief Instructor of the Japan Karate Association. A few years later, when I was training at the JKA headquarters in Tokyo, I took many incredible lessons under his instruction.

At that moment, though, with Dayo standing in front of me, I wasn't thinking about who was watching. I just wanted to kick off!

The wife of one of our team, a good guy called Jim O'Grady, said to her husband, 'Jim, I wish you had friends like that. If it kicks off in here, you back Dave up!'

I know he would have done, but I saw reason and nothing happened. Not then.

I waited until the end of the competition before seeing Dayo again. I'd been rooming with my very good friend Billy Higgins and, once our bags were packed and we were ready to leave, I asked him if he'd mind keeping his eye on my case, because there was someone I needed to say goodbye to. I went straight to Dayo's room and, when he opened the door, I gave him Tony's regards. Then I gave him some of mine! When I got back home I informed Tony that Dayo and I had met. Tony didn't say much, but he did have a very wide smile on his face.

A few years later, Tony phoned me. He said, 'What do you think of Ee-ee?'

I said, 'Who the fuck is that?'

He said, 'You know, Ee-ee. She's just got to number one in the charts.'

I hadn't got a clue who he was talking about.

Tony said, 'Do you remember the young girl we taught at Goldsmiths, who we used to call "Ee-ee"?'

I said, 'Oh, yeah. The one who used to squeak when

she *kiaied*. I remember her now.'

Tony said, 'Well, what's her name?'

I said, 'Katy.'

He said, 'That's right. And what's her brother's name – the black belt?'

'Bush. Dr John Bush.'

'So what's her full name, then?'

'Katy Bush.' Then I realised. 'Kate Bush! Ee-ee is Kate Bush!'

She'd just got to number one with her song *Wuthering Heights*. I watched her perform it on TV. There she was, little Ee-ee, singing, 'Heathcliff it's me... come home.' Interestingly, it looked to me as if some of her dance moves were a bit like karate techniques. Of course, Katy went on to become really, really successful. I was so pleased for her – and pissed off for myself because she didn't ask me to be Heathcliff!

Chapter 26

'HE'S A BIT FLIGHTY'

One night a boxer visited the Marshall Street *dojo*. He was a big, loud lump, who told all the beginners that he'd come to bash the karate instructor. I rushed out of the changing rooms and saw Sensei walking towards the boxer. I immediately ran after him – as if Sensei needed me to protect him! Anyway, before I knew it he'd grabbed this lump by the scruff of the neck and slapped him – bang, crash, wallop! – with the front and the back of his hand, as if he were a naughty boy. In doing so he knocked him absolutely cold. As I reached Sensei he threw the boxer at me. He was three times bigger than me and bowled me over. Sensei, on the other hand, had just handled him like a rag doll.

He said, 'Dabie, throw him out! Take downstairs and throw out, but, please, not too much damage – bad publicity.'

The problem was, Marshall Street *dojo* was at the top of a leisure centre. It had so many sets of stairs it was untrue, and I'd got to get this lump all the way down and into the street!

I set off, carrying him on my shoulders. I was in my karate *gi* and he, obviously, was in civvies. It wasn't long before I felt him starting to come round.

I thought, This could get nasty. He's just been slapped all over the place and now all he'll see is a little bloke taking him downstairs to throw him out.

I moved as quickly as I could, but by the time I was halfway down the stairs he wanted to fight again. Now, I'm not Enoeda Sensei. I couldn't just slap him a couple of times and send him back to sleep. I'd got to get ugly and hurt the fucker. So I did!

You've got to put what happened next into context. I'd arranged to meet a couple of good karate friends of mine, Bob Waterhouse and Dave Vaughn, after training, and they were going to introduce me to their wives. They'd already told them, 'Dave's OK, but he's a bit flighty. When you watch him train it can get a bit spiteful.'

So there I was, getting into this boxer big time, giving him plenty of big digs – we were both covered in claret – when suddenly I hear 'tap, tap, tap' coming up the stairs. It was Bob and Dave with their wives. These women had been told that I could get out of my pram sometimes, and, sure enough, the first time they see me I'm bashing this guy on the stairs!

I stopped for a second and said, 'Hello, Bob, hello, Dave – I'll be with ya in a minute,' and then went back to work on the boxer. The two women kept as far away from me they could, but they still had to walk through the bits and pieces.

Eventually, I got this fella on the street, left him there and went back up to Sensei. He saw I was covered in blood and said, 'Look at the state of your *gi*. What happened?'

I said, 'Sorry, Sensei, but halfway down he woke up.'

'Really?'

'Yeah. I calmed him down a bit and then got rid of him.'

'Where?'

'Outside. On the kerb.'

'No problem?'

'No, Sensei. No problem.'

Sensei nodded. 'There is one problem. You look disgraceful. You have to leave now. Shower and go home. Bad manners looking like that.'

I had a quick shower and went out for dinner with Bob and Dave and their wives. Of course, the women wouldn't talk to me or look at me. I don't think they did for at least a year. They just thought of me as a violent little bugger. What they didn't realise was that if I hadn't clumped the guy he would have mullered me!

Chapter 27

FIGHTING

*A*s a kid, I grew up fighting. It was inevitable in the environment that I lived in that you'd get into scraps. It wasn't life-or-death stuff, just silly, pushing, shoving and slapping. I was quite an angelic-looking kid (you wouldn't believe it now!) and I've never been big, so a lot of times I'd get into a conflict because I looked an easy target.

The fact that I don't look like the sort of person who can handle himself is a factor that's run through my martial-arts career. A lot of people wear their threat on the outside. I like to think I carry mine on the inside. It still seems to blow people away when they discover you've got a level of performance they didn't expect.

On the street, in my normal daily life, I don't want anyone to recognise what I can do. If someone wants to fight me for real, I don't want them to spot what they're *up against – not until I've knocked them out! Do I tell them I do karate when they threaten or challenge me? Only when they're unconscious!*

On the street I don't want people to read me. When I'm teaching in the dojo, when I've put my gi and belt on, it's a different matter. Then I can be more obvious. Then I want those who haven't trained with me before to sense something that I usually keep well hidden. And I want those who have trained with me before to <u>remember</u>.

Chapter 28

BIG-TIME BUSY IN JAPAN

Before I went to Japan I always modelled my karate on Enoeda Sensei. I wanted to be just like him, which, given that he was a mature man and built like a tank and I was a young man built like a potato chip, was never going to happen. Sensei advised me, 'Don't copy me. Copy someone who is built like you. When you are in Japan look at Yahara.'

I did, and I realised very quickly that Yahara Sensei had a very special talent. The first time I saw him it was obvious he was a special sort of mover and I worked to emulate him. Incredibly, it just so happened that he liked the way I moved, too, and picked me as one of his trainees. That meant, among other things, that we got to fight on a daily basis. I was really fit at the time – I was training six or seven hours a day – and so was he. Some days we fought tooth and nail for twenty-five minutes without stopping. I'd have just finished an hour and a half class and was going to do a two-hour instructor's class later in the day, but it didn't matter. Nothing mattered. I was living for the moment and gave it everything I'd got.

I flew out to Japan in 1977 with my good friend Ray Kerridge. We had no real idea what we were getting ourselves into. Would we be surrounded by *samurai* or businessmen who worked for Toyota? All I knew was that I wanted to experience karate training at the source. I didn't go there looking for better instruction. How could I? In my eyes, the greatest *karateka* on the planet, Enoeda Sensei, was living in London. No, I went there to test myself in a different way and to absorb the Japanese experience. As it happens I did have the privilege of training regularly under the man who was, arguably, the greatest karate instructor ever, Enoeda Sensei's instructor, Master Nakayama. I'll tell you more about him later.

Once we got off the plane we went straight to the JKA headquarters in Ebisu, Tokyo. We introduced ourselves to Tagaki Sensei, paid our subscription for the *gaijin* class (*gaijin* means 'alien' in Japanese) and were invited to train straight away. Afterwards, we met Dave Hooper, an English *karateka*, who let us stay with him for a few days until we got ourselves sorted out.

People were always coming and going at the JKA. When we arrived, a Portuguese student was in the process of leaving and we were able to rent his place. It was a very small, six-*tatami* room. One *tatami* (which is Japanese floor matting, and rooms are traditionally measured by the number of *tatami* mats that will fit in) is about six feet by two and half feet in size, so although this was called a room there wasn't actually much room in it. In one corner there was a recess containing a sink and a little hot plate. A cupboard at one end housed our clothes and our rolled-up futons, or bedding. The toilet was outside the room, at the end of the corridor. It was a traditional Japanese toilet, which meant that you had to squat over the 'crap plate', as we called it. We shared this with a Japanese couple who lived in the one other room off our landing. There was no shower or bath, but that was OK because we could either shower at the JKA, or go the public, communal bath house, or *sento*, as it is called.

Essentially, Ray and I had found ourselves a traditional little Japanese dwelling and, better still, it was only a ten-minute walk from the JKA. We loved it!

Ray actually visited the *sento* before me and, when he returned, he was grinning from ear to ear.

'You have to go,' he said. 'You'll really like it.'

I thought he meant you could get a peek at the women, but I was to be disappointed on that score. Men and women had separate changing rooms and the main room itself had a large partition down the middle, with men bathing on one side and women on the other. The idea was that you sat on a stool near a tap and washed yourself spotless. Then there was a choice of three hot tubs that you could sit and soak in for as long as you could stand it. The first tub was just hot. The second tub was very hot, and the third tub was burn-your-balls-off hot. Going to the *sento* was a social event and many of the Japanese would spend up to a couple of hours in there.

What had amused Ray so much was the Japanese men's

reaction to him as he walked naked around the *sento*. Ray was well hung and the size of his 'best friend' had come as quite a shock to his fellow bathers, many of whom had stared and pointed as he walked past. You have to remember that, generally speaking, Japanese men are smaller in stature than Brits – and every part of them is in proportion, if you get my meaning. Nothing, it seems, had prepared them for the sight of Ray's tackle, and he thought it would be great fun if, the next time he went for a public bath, I went with him. I agreed, foolishly. I say 'foolishly' because I'm not well hung. Ray, though, had the solution.

'All you have to do,' he said, as we undressed in the *sento*'s changing rooms, 'is slap yourself around a bit. Give yourself a "lazy lob". That's what I did last time and it scared them to death!'

By then I was giggling so much that I couldn't do anything and, sad to say, when I walked in to the baths, no one gave me a second glance.

As I'm sure you've realised, our flat was hardly big enough for two grown men to live in. What made it bearable was the fact that we spent most of our time training at the JKA, so we used the flat primarily as a place to sleep. What made it almost unbearable was the fact that, as naturally generous guys, we always invited people to stay if they needed to. Within a couple of months of moving in we'd got two South Africans, Keith Geyer and Tase Matasan, both over six foot tall and three foot wide, living with us. Things became even more crowded when the world champs came around and Mick Dewey and Bob Waterhouse came over from England and moved in, too. Now the room that was barely large enough to accommodate two grown men was home to six! At night we slept like sardines.

1977 was Jubilee year. My Mum sent over some Jubilee flags and all the paraphernalia that went with them, and we used these to decorate the room. For the most part, I didn't allow myself to think about my family during my time in Japan. It would have done my head in. After all, when you're away from home and you're under duress, where is it you most want to be? Back home, of course. If I'd let myself think like that, I'd have ended up pulling my head off! What helped, too, was that I didn't have to worry about my family's safety while I was away. I'd asked Dave Robinson to give them a call every now and then just to make sure they were OK. I knew if any problems arose he'd take care of them.

After I'd been in Japan for a few months I decided to phone home just the once, just to let Mum know I was all right. Of course, I also asked her how they were.

'Everything's fine,' she said. 'And isn't Dave Robinson a lovely man? He's so funny, too.'

'Is he?'

'Oh, yes. We always share the same little joke every time he phones.'

'What joke is that, Mum?'

'When he's asked if everything is all right, he always says, "So, is there anyone you want shot this week, Mrs Hazard?" How funny is that? It always makes me giggle.'

'You haven't given him anyone's name as a joke, have you, Mum?'

'Of course not. Why?'

'I think the joke would backfire, Mum. Whatever you do, don't say anyone's name.'

Every Friday night we'd buy a couple of litre bottles of cheap *sake*, the famous Japanese rice wine, and some cheese. We'd have a bowl of noodles, then drink the *sake* and eat the cheese. After that, we'd get down to the serious business of singing. We sang a medley of songs by the Beatles and John Denver, who was Ray's favourite artist. We always finished with *God Save the Queen*. The South Africans weren't too happy about that, but, as they were staying in our home, they didn't have a choice!

One night, when we were all pickled, I decided to play some music for us to go to sleep to. Mick, being equally drunk, slurred, 'Put Lenny Benim on.'

Now, you may be wondering who Lenny Benim is. If you're unsure it's probably because you're sober. In my drunken state I knew exactly who Mick was talking about, even though I'd never heard the name before. He was trying to say the name of one of my favourite musicians, George Benson. How I actually made the connection between the two I've no idea, but from that day to this George Benson has always been Lenny Benim to Mick and me!

Another regular visitor to our humble abode was a Scotsman, Ronnie Ross. We first met at the *gaijin* class at the JKA, where Ronnie was quick to introduce himself. I think he was pleased to have two more guys from back home to train with.

When we first arrived, the *gaijin* class was unofficially controlled by a group of French *karateka*.

They were arrogant bullies who needed to be taught some manners, and Ray and I were just the boys to do it! We taught the French some manners in a manner that they would never forget. Actually, we taught them such good manners that, after we had hammered home the most important points, they left the class and never came back! From that moment on, the *gaijin* class became really nice to train in. We made sure that it stayed that way, too.

Ronnie Ross is a very good *karateka* and an even better friend. He saved my bacon a few times when I was really tight for money or food. Lack of food was one of the great challenges I faced – that and the heat.

Many people have asked me what the food was like in Japan. The truth is, I've eaten better Japanese food in England than I ever did over there. Then I simply couldn't afford to eat well. Ray and me lived on noodle soup and the occasional Big Mac, and that would be our one meal for the day. It was no wonder I lost weight! It does make you realise, though, how little food your body actually needs, and how much food we waste here in the West.

The training regime I followed was as tough as it gets. Knowing that you are going to be training three times a day, and that in one of those sessions – the instructor's class – you are going to be surrounded by the very best in the world who will take no prisoners, is emotionally draining. Actually putting yourself through it, day after day, is both physically and mentally exhausting. When you add into the equation the fact that the temperature and humidity were much higher than I was used to, and that most of the time I was starving, you can begin to appreciate how difficult things were.

Ronnie lived in a three-and-a-half-*tatami* room, a space just large enough for one person. He lived alone, which was just as well because the room was filled with boxes and boxes of coloured beads and wire. They'd been left behind by the previous tenant and Ronnie used them to set up a little business. He would sit up all night making necklaces and trinkets, which he'd then sell at the train station.

He was also very good at a Japanese game called *pachinko*. Imagine a pinball machine standing upright and you'll get the idea. The aim was to flick ball bearings, which you had to buy, into the holes on the board. Each hole had a different value, and the higher your score, the more ball bearings you got back in return. At the end of the game you returned any ball bearings you had won and received tokens that you could exchange for soap and cigarettes – things like that. Ronnie was so good at this that he always finished with a load of ball bearings. Better still, he had reached an agreement with the guy in charge, who gave him money back instead of tokens. In this way Ronnie made himself a living and was able to help me out when I needed it. Sometimes he'd buy me dinner. We'd eat *shabu-shabu*, which is a hotpot of meat and vegetables. After living off noodles and the occasional burger, this was like a banquet.

To anyone who knows Ronnie, it will come as no surprise that he coped so well in Japan. He is a most talented man, a singer and musician, who can turn his hand to anything. It's been a privilege for me to teach at his *dojo*, and visit him and his family three times a year for the last twenty years.

I did a few odd jobs in Japan, too. I didn't have a choice. I hadn't taken enough money to fund my stay, so I had to find ways to earn an income. I worked in a restaurant, washing dishes, and I worked in a coffee shop, clearing up. I also got some work teaching English. Don't laugh! It may be true that I have, on occasion, had trouble spelling 'Hazard', but you have to remember that this was 1977. The Japanese didn't want to learn how to write in English, just how to have a conversation. As a Cockney, I certainly knew how to talk, even if I didn't always use the Queen's English.

The teaching method was very basic. Students were required to read out loud from a couple of books and I had to tell them whether or not they were saying the words correctly. Although this sounds simple, I very quickly developed a fallback position in case my limited skills were stretched past their limit. I identified the brightest spark in the class and, if I was ever asked a question I didn't know the answer to, I'd turn to him and ask him what he thought.

We'd usually begin each class working from the reading books, but after a while they'd be forgotten as we found ourselves chatting about all sorts of things. More often than not I'd end up teaching them my speciality, Cockney rhyming slang.

The group was always very small – there were never more than eight students – so when we had a good conversation going I'd suggest that we continue it in the local coffee shop. They always agreed and, thankfully, someone always bought me a coffee – which, even in those days, cost the equivalent of £2! I thought this was one of my better plans until, one day, we were en route to the coffee shop when the Head of School walked past. He was clearly unhappy about what he regarded as my needless change of venue. He became even less happy when a car drove by and one my students said to me, 'Sensei! Sensei, look! A jam jar going down the frog and toad!'

I saw a look of horror cross the Head's face and, before he could say anything, I turned to the group. 'C'mon! Quickly!' I shouted. 'Move your plates of meat! Let's get out of here!'

I still wonder if any of my students ever used the language I taught them in later life – at a business conference maybe.

All the work I did was 'black work'. In other words, it was technically illegal. I didn't have a work permit, only a visitor's visa, so I was always paid in cash. I earned enough to survive. Just. People were generous and all of us who were in the same boat looked after each other the best we could. It's a funny thing, how, when you've got sod all, you're so willing to give it away. But that's how it was. Friendships formed very quickly, partly because we were under so much pressure and partly because we respected the sacrifices we were all making.

Every time someone was preparing to leave, we'd hold a *sayonara* party (*sayonara* is the Japanese equivalent of our 'goodbye'). With me, Ray, Mick Dewey, Bob Waterhouse, Keith and Tase living in a six-*tatami* space, our place was the place to be for parties!

One night, during a *sayonara* party, a group of Japanese gathered outside complaining about the noise and wanting to know how we could get so many people into such a small room. Eventually, they sent a representative to knock on our door and ask for some peace and quiet. It was an understandable request and one that we honoured.

I was far less understanding with the chickens that moved in across the road. There were six of them in a recess between the buildings, with a little wire fence to keep them in. And they were loud. Very loud. Every morning at five o'clock I was woken by the rooster's 'Cock-a-doodle-fucking-do!' I was always tired and hungry. I was often injured. The last thing I needed was an early-morning call. People who choose to live in the countryside accept that they're going to be woken at sunrise every day by the coos, calls, screams and squawks of a range of animals and birds. That's the price you pay for country life. It's not what you expect in the city. I couldn't for the life of me work out why some Japanese guy had suddenly decided to play at being a farmer in the middle of Tokyo! Whatever his misguided reasons, it didn't take long for me to start hating those chickens. Don't get me wrong here, I am an animal lover – I have to be because half of my mates are animals (only joking) – but there is a time and place for all things.

If you are a chicken 5am is definitely not the best time to interrupt my sleep when I'm training five or six hours a day with some of the most dangerous men on the planet. And living right outside my bedroom window is not the best place to be. I'll tell you why. First, it makes it far too easy for you to upset me and, second, it makes it far too easy for me to return the compliment! Which is exactly what I planned to do.

Coping with the demands of the JKA and the instructor's class every day was pushing me to my limit. Chickens were the final straw. They didn't know it – hey, chickens are so stupid that if you chop their head off they still run around until one of their mates tells them they're dead – but they'd created a problem that was coming home to roost. It was going to be me or them! But it never reached that stage. It seems that at least one other local city dweller felt the same as I did about this countryside invasion. The story I heard was that a bottle of bleach was poured into the chickens' water trough, just to help them clear their throats, so to speak. The next morning, all was quiet on the Eastern front. Fucking lovely! Now all I had to do was concentrate on my training.

The JKA *dojo* in Tokyo was the best *dojo* in the world. It was a huge, converted bowling alley. There were lots of mirrors on one wall and there was a very heavy leather bag hanging from the ceiling. At one end there was a box with the flags of all the countries affiliated to the JKA sticking out of it. One day, Yahara Sensei and me were scrapping – we'd been going at it for quite a time, banging each other off different walls and stuff – when he caught me with an almighty kick that knocked me straight through the flag box and onto the floor. I wasn't badly hurt, but I did think, Jesus! That's spiteful. I'll have a bit of a deep breath before I get back up.

Now, you need to understand that, in the culture of the *dojo*, the worst thing that could happen to a trainee instructor like me was being floored by a senior who then walked away. If they did that it meant they were disgusted with you – either because you hadn't given them enough of a scrap or because they just didn't like you. Yahara Sensei was a hero to most people over there and, as he was my senior instructor, I thought a great deal of him as

131

well. The last thing I wanted was for him ever to turn his back on me and walk away, so every time we fought I gave him everything I'd got.

This time, though, it seemed that I'd got it wrong. By the time I'd had a couple of breaths and jumped back to my feet the *dojo* was deserted. My heart sank. What have I done? I asked myself as I climbed out through the flag box. He's actually left me. He's given me a clump and left me. It's the biggest insult.

At that moment a foot appeared from nowhere and hit me – smack! – straight in the face. It was Yahara, lying on the floor behind the box. I was so relieved that I didn't notice the pain. He was in fits of laughter.

'You thought I'd left you!' he said. 'You thought I'd left you, but I didn't. Ha! Ha! Ha! I stayed here to kick you in the face!'

How's that for a compliment?

Another time when we were fighting he swept me to the floor and I grabbed his foot as he tried to kick me.

'Now what?' he asked.

'I don't understand,' I said.

'Bite it!' He ordered. 'Bite it!'

So I started biting his ankle and he promptly kicked me with his other foot! 'Idea is good! Idea is good!' he said. 'One day it might save your life.'

As I've said, Yahara Sensei was special, but so were the all the other senior instructors. The head of the Japan Karate Association and the Chief Instructor was Master Nakayama. He led a list that today sounds like a who's who of karate. When I was there, the sensei who were either teaching or training in the class on a regular basis included Kanazawa, Shoji, Asai, Ueki,

Yamaguchi, Abe, Oishi, Tanaka, Yahara, Iida, Osaka and many others who went on to become world-famous instructors. Training with them every day in the instructors' class was always very demanding. The class was about thirty strong and was affectionately known as 'the Hornets' Nest'. It was made up of the aforementioned Sensei plus those students thought to have the potential to become instructors. These usually came from the top university clubs and, if they made it through to the end of the three-year course, they qualified as JKA instructors.

Normally each trainee was taken under the wing of one of the seniors, who would then help them through the programme. Mind you, whether they were helped or hindered depended on which senior picked you. For example, Tanaka Sensei was a notoriously hard taskmaster. He was about five foot ten tall, which is quite tall for a Japanese. He was well muscled with a shaven head, a thin, black moustache and a face that could curdle milk with a single glance. He had won just about every title there was to win, including the JKA World Championships. Once, when one of his charges was late for a class, he punched his front teeth out.

He did once make a small error of judgement, though, when he roughed up the trainee of Osaka Sensei. Now, Osaka was the total opposite of Tanaka. Don't get me wrong, he was as hard as nails and his technique was world-renowned – if Master Nakayama wanted something demonstrated, he would get Osaka to show it – but I never saw him bully anyone. Anyway, Osaka entered the *dojo* to see his boy black and blue, with blood running from his mouth and both eyes closing rapidly.

He didn't say a word. The class began and we went through our normal routine of a warm-up, basic movements and then fighting. After about an hour and a half of this, Master Nakayama stopped the training and called everyone round for our usual one-on-one in front of the class.

Normally, one of the instructors would be up first. He'd dish out some pain to two or three of the trainees, then another instructor would replace him and do the same to a few more. On this occasion, Tanaka was first up and, to everyone's surprise, Osaka jumped up to face him! To be honest, I thought that Osaka Sensei had made a bit of a mistake, because although he was very, very good, Tanaka was a nightmare! And he'd cheat to make a point! For example, when you did prearranged sparring with him and you were supposed to attack five times, he would attack six or seven. Just when you thought it was over, in would come his little extra! So, as I watched this, I was fearing for Osaka. It was the first time I'd ever seen an instructor get up in place of a trainee. As Osaka and Tanaka faced each other, you could have cut the atmosphere in the *dojo* with a knife

Master Nakayama said, '*Hajime*!' ('Start!') and – bang, bang! – it was all over in a second! It was that quick! I was in shock and I'm sure a few others were, too, but no one was more shocked than Tanaka. Osaka Sensei's kick hit him, like lightning, in the stomach and, as his feet were coming off the floor, his punch caught him right between the eyes. Tanaka Sensei landed with a thump, but was back up in an instant. Osaka's control had been perfect – just enough to take Tanaka's balance with the kick and just enough on the punch to let him know that he'd been there. Then, with a polite little bow he shuffled back to his place – no arrogance, no attitude, just a quick rub on the head of his trainee as he passed him. What a class act!

The fact that I'd been invited into the instructors' class was quite unusual for that time and, although it could get very, very spiteful, I didn't do too badly overall. Mind you, I was wearing Enoeda Sensei's belt and there was no way I was going to let him down.

I'll never forget the day he walked into the *dojo* between classes. He'd come over to Japan with the British squad for the World Championships. I knew he was around, but I didn't expect to see him then. There was a forty-five-minute break between the class that had just finished and the one that was due to start, and the rule was that if you were in the *dojo* you had to keep busy. You couldn't take a rest or stand around talking. If you did, one of the seniors would immediately order you to spar with him – and that could get spiteful. So the trainee instructors always made sure that they were doing something useful. We'd be stretching or working on a particular technique or hitting the *makiwara* (punching boards). While we were doing that, the seniors would stroll around watching us, looking for someone who didn't seem busy enough.

Anyway, during this particular break I was on the floor stretching, and seniors such as Yahara Sensei and Tanaka Sensei were giving us all the evil eye, looking for a victim, and all of a sudden the door opened and Enoeda Sensei walked in. Well! You should have seen those senior instructors get busy! They went from strolling around to big-time busy in a split second!

Enoeda Sensei began doing some stretching himself,

but all the while he was looking around at the senior instructors and no one, absolutely no one, made eye contact with him! I was so chuffed because now my Boss was in there and everyone was being as busy as I was. After a few minutes he began doing some kicks in front of the mirrors and it was just phenomenal! Whoosh! Whoosh!

Then he turned round and started working on the leather bag. I'd worked on this bag a lot, and so had everyone else. We all knew how heavy it was. Enoeda Sensei just pushed the bag away from him and, as it swung back, he went bang! with this incredible kick. The bag just cut itself in half with the power he put into it, and split wide open. I don't know whether the bag had been weakened by the wear and tear it had already taken, but I do know that he wiped it out.

Sensei then did a couple more kicks towards the mirror, looked round the *dojo* again and went, 'Huh!' as if to say, 'That's right, make sure you keep busy. The old Master has returned.' Then he left the *dojo*. It was obvious that he'd just blown everyone away. They were scared to death of him and, boy, did I strut that day!

Chapter 29

BATS, BAR GIRLS AND A CURFEW IN KOREA

The only time I ever got to travel through Japan during my year there was a five-day period when I had to stop training to go and renew my visa. It should have taken me only two days to do that but me, silly bollocks, looked at the map and decided that it would be easy to collect my visa and then get a boat over to Korea. I'd figured that it would take only one day to travel to the port, but it ended up taking me nearly three. It wasn't just because I had to hitch rides that I was delayed. My big mistake was in not appreciating how long the actual journey was. On the map it didn't look too far. In reality it was a winding, long and slow road. I set off with a change of jeans, some T-shirts and very little else.

On the first night, I slept underneath a little rowing boat on a beach. There are loads of bats on the Japanese coast and, as I tried to sleep, I could hear them flying out to sea. I never heard them return for one very simple reason – they never did return. You see, while the Japanese clearly love their chickens (well, some of them do, anyway), they definitely don't appreciate bats. Rows of poles had been placed along the coastline and each pole emitted a sound that, to bats, was like a brick wall. This meant that whenever they began to fly back to shore they thought they were in danger of flying into something solid, so they'd turn round and fly back out to sea. After a while they'd realise there was nowhere for them to go and they'd try to come back to land again, only to hear the noise and be forced to turn back. The poor little fuckers kept going backwards and forwards until they became exhausted, fell into the sea and drowned.

The Japanese are very helpful people, but if they don't like you they can be a bit spiteful.

The port I travelled to, Shimonoseki, is on the south coast of Japan. From there I got a boat to Pusan in Korea. I planned to spend a couple of hours wandering around – I just wanted to say I'd been really – and then catch the next boat back. The boat I went on was crammed. This was the poor person's way of getting to Korea. There was a large *tatami* floor area where the passengers sat for the duration of the voyage. If you moved away from your space there was a chance that someone else would steal it, so you stayed put.

What I didn't know until I arrived in Korea was that, once you were there, you had to stay for a minimum of twenty-four hours. It was a moneymaking ploy, but unfortunately for the Korean economy – and for me, as it would turn out – I'd hardly got any cash with me.

I spent what I'd got in a seedy little bar on the docks. It sold noodles, beer and women, not necessarily in that order. I ordered something from the menu that looked like a type of noodle soup, realised that I couldn't afford a beer to go with it and, when one of the bar girls approached me, I smiled politely and said, 'Thanks, but no, thanks. I'm broke.'

I don't think she understood a single word I said, but no is a pretty easy message to convey in any language. She nodded, smiled in return, and left me alone.

While I waited for my food, I looked round the room. It was like something from a cowboy film, with a wooden bar and wooden stools. It was certainly not the sort of place you'd take your girlfriend for a date. The guy, who I assumed was the owner, brought me a beer with my noodle soup. I told him that I couldn't afford to pay for it. He shrugged and told me to drink it anyway. I did. As soon as I'd finished, he bought me another one. I thought, What the hell's going on here? Will he be saucy and try to charge me for the drinks?

No matter. I had my second beer, then prepared to pay for my soup and leave. In his very limited English the guy told me that I couldn't go.

'Why not?' I asked, ready to clump him if necessary.

He explained that there was a curfew and I'd be shot if I went outside. He said that I could pay to sleep in the bar. I reminded him that I had no money. At that moment three of his mates appeared from the backroom. Things were suddenly not looking too good. The last thing I wanted was get into a fight with these guys. Even if I beat them, then what? I couldn't go anywhere until the morning.

The owner was thoughtful for a moment, then he picked up my bag and took out my jeans and T-shirts as payment. Much as it annoyed me, I stood back and let him. Satisfied that he'd got all he could, he returned to the backroom with his friends, where they drank beer and played cards for most of the night. Eventually, I fell asleep in the bar.

I was woken early in the morning by the girl who had approached me. I don't know what her name was, but I'll always remember her face. She signalled for me to keep quiet, gave me my clothes back, which she had folded neatly, and let me out.

I can't imagine what would have happened if I'd still been there when the owner and his mates reappeared. My guess is that we wouldn't have shared a jolly breakfast together, or made plans to meet up again. Looking back on it, I think my beautiful Korean bar girl saved a lot more than just my clothes!

I took the boat back to Shimonoseki and hitched to Osaka. A very famous British martial artist, Terry Wingrove, lived there. I found his house and sat on the doorstep from 6.30 till 8 a.m., when I thought they'd be up. Then I knocked on the door. Terry gave me breakfast, took me to the train station and even bought me a ticket for the bullet train. Instead of taking a day to hitch back to Tokyo, I was there within a few hours.

Chapter 30

A GIANT AND A GENIUS

I'd been given permission by Master Nakayama, the Head of the JKA, to go and renew my visa, but, even so, I knew that I was in for a hard time when I returned to the instructors' class. The rule was very simple – you had to attend every session. If you were ill you had to turn up and, if it was decided that you couldn't train, you'd be sent home again. If you were too injured to train, you either had to be in the hospital or turn up and watch. The rest of the time you had to train. So, even though everyone knew that I needed to renew my visa, even though Master Nakayama had OK'd my absence, I was still pushed around harder than normal on my first lesson back.

It was inevitable, given the ferocity of the training, that people were injured. Sometimes the damage was caused intentionally. Sometimes it was an accident. If you were in the instructors' class you had to become good quickly, because hospital treatment in Japan was very expensive and the JKA paid only for your first two visits. After that, you had to fund the money yourself. Given that I could barely afford to eat, I simply had to make sure that wasn't hospitalised more than twice.

During one class, Iida Sensei broke a couple of my ribs with a well-delivered front kick. There was no malice in what he did. I failed to block correctly and paid the inevitable price. Iida Sensei was a large man, built like the Buddha, and was a very, very good *karateka*. One year he actually won the All-Japan All-Styles championships. He was also a nice guy and he apologised for injuring me, even though he didn't need to. If you're learning to fight you have to expect to get hit. In most things, if you make a mistake there's an inevitable consequence. In what I do, the inevitable consequence is a clump. It's that simple.

The next day I was back in the class. My ribs were tightly strapped and my movements were quite restricted. Master Nakayama checked me out before the lesson began. When he saw the extent of my injury he told me to train only gently and to sit down during the *kumite*, or sparring, part of the class. It was wise advice. Another kick, or even a punch, into my broken ribs could have caused serious, possibly even fatal, damage.

The class started with the usual *kihon*, or basic, techniques. It wasn't long before I started getting some sideways glances from the instructors who were training around me. I could see them thinking, Why is he going so slowly? Why is he being so careful?

Of course, only Master Nakayama and Iida Sensei knew of my injury, so in the eyes of everyone else I was just not doing a very good job. Still, I carried on the best I could. When the *kihon* was over, Master Nakayama told everyone to pair up. It was time for some sparring. Suddenly, I realised my predicament. I was in a class with thirty superstars, none of whom had heard Master Nakayama tell me to sit out. I hesitated. To be honest, I didn't want them to think I was bottling it for some reason.

In 'the Hornets' Nest' the worst thing you could do was hesitate. A split second later one of the instructors was in front of me. It was Tabata Sensei, one of Enoeda Sensei's main students, and the biggest man in the *dojo*. He was a phenomenal *karateka*, a very nice guy, and a giant. He turned to face me with a broad smile on his face – he smiled at everyone – and I glanced at his huge hands and feet. Outside the *dojo* this man was a gentle giant, but inside he could hold his own with anyone.

I thought to myself, If he hits me in the body I'm in serious, serious trouble.

We bowed and, at Master Nakayama's command, began sparring.

It didn't last very long. The first thing Tabata Sensei did was to sweep both my feet from under me. My body flew upwards – at one point I was horizontal to the floor – and his leg traced a big arc through the air, following me down as I began my descent. Hitting the floor was bad enough with my broken ribs, but the sight of his size-eleven foot coming down at lightning speed to stamp on my chest was even worse. While I had no doubt that Tabata Sensei would control the impact of his kick, I also knew that the normal level of contact permitted in the class was far more than I could currently take. I prepared myself for the worst.

In that instant, I heard Master Nakayama's voice shout, *Yame*! – 'Stop!' – and Tabata Sensei's foot froze in midair, inches above my ribs. It was the most amazing display of self-control! By the time he had returned his foot to the floor, Master Nakayama had rushed over. He hadn't realised that I'd joined in the *kumite* until he'd seen Tabata Sensei take my feet away.

I got a bit of a bollocking for ignoring Master Nakayama's instruction to sit down during the *kumite*, but poor old Tabata Sensei got an almighty telling-off. Which, I have to say, seemed a bit unfair given that I hadn't told him about my injury. It was rather funny, though, watching this huge man standing there, with his head bowed like a naughty schoolboy, while his tiny teacher bollocked him rigid.

The instructors' class at the JKA was like life itself. Master Nakayama explained to us once that some *dojos* were too austere, and created students who were too fearful to learn well. Other *dojos* were too relaxed and, in those, students failed to develop self-discipline or the fighting spirit. He said that the best *dojos* reflected all of life. Students should enjoy their training, yet take it seriously. Training should be hard and challenging at times, but if something happens that is funny you should be able to smile and enjoy it. After all, students pay to be taught in the *dojo*. They are willing conscripts and even people in the army laugh sometimes.

The truth is that, wherever you are, whether it's in different cultures, groups or even just families, you'll meet some lovely people and you'll meet some arseholes. It was the same in the JKA. People like Osaka Sensei, Iida Sensei and Tabata Sensei were wonderful human beings. And Master Nakayama was very special indeed. He was an amazing teacher. He could watch you do a technique once and then tell you exactly what to do to improve it. He was only a tiny man, whom I never saw being even remotely spiteful, but he taught, controlled and led some of the best *karateka* the world has ever seen. He was a great technician as well as a great instructor. If any *karateka* I've ever met was worthy of the title 'Master', it was him. Only him. He was a giant and a genius.

PART 3

RONIN
(*Ronin*: a masterless *samurai*)
1978-1985

Chapter 31

'YOU DIDN'T TELL US YOU WERE COMING HOME'

I didn't tell anyone that I was coming back to England. As it happened, though, my timing was perfect, because when I got back to my parents' place, Mum had gone to collect Tracey from school. That meant I had the flat to myself for a while. I put my bag in the kitchen and sat there, waiting. When they came back I heard the usual things in the hall.

Mum saying, 'Tracey, get your shoes off.'

Tracey saying, 'I'm just going to get a drink.'

And then in she came, my beautiful eight-year-old sister, not expecting to see anyone there, let alone me. When she saw me sitting there she froze. I put my finger to my mouth, telling her to keep quiet, and then beckoned for her to come to me. She jumped on my lap, hugged me and sat there, sobbing.

The next minute we heard Mum's voice from the

bedroom. 'Tracey, come here. You need to get your school clothes off and in the wash.'

Tracey didn't move.

'Tracey! Come here!'

I could hear Mum getting irritated now.

'Tracey! Do as you're told!'

There was no chance of that happening and, a few seconds later, Mum marched into the kitchen. She saw me and stopped dead. She stared at me in silence for a few seconds and then said, 'You didn't tell us you were coming home.' Her hands flapped in front of her as she spoke. 'You didn't tell us!' And, with that, she turned and ran into her bedroom.

'Thanks, Mum!' I shouted after her. 'That's a nice welcome!' Which, of course, it was.

For the next few days, after Mum had dropped Tracey off at school, she would buy us both a doughnut each from the cake shop – she'd get the one with more icing sugar on it for me – and then the pair of us would sit together talking, eating our cakes and enjoying a cup of tea. It wasn't long, though, before she came back with two doughnuts and two iced buns each. Then it became three of everything, then four! It was the only form of motherly love that I've ever had to put a stop to – although it wasn't the only time that Mum and I have been a bit silly where food's concerned.

We share a devilish sense of humour, so sometimes our games would get out of hand. You've probably heard someone say that they've laughed so much that it hurt. Well, on one occasion when Mum and I were playing jokes on each other in the kitchen, I ended up hurting so much that I laughed.

I've taken a lot of hits in my life, but I've only ever been knocked out twice. The first time it was at the hands – well, actually, if you remember, it was by the feet – of Enoeda Sensei, after I'd ruined the drive up to Liverpool. So, no disgrace there, then. The second time, I was dropped by a loaf of bread. Nowadays some people think that white bread is bad for you. Well I know for a fact that it is! Especially when it's frozen solid and swung full force into the back of your unsuspecting neck! If you're wondering just what sort of person would use their loaf like that to hurt someone as lovable as me, well, I'll tell you. It was my best friend – my beautiful, mischievous Mum!

It all started when we were making sandwiches and tea together. Although I was 27 years old, I still had a silly, schoolboy habit of stirring my tea and then touching anyone who was near me on the back of their hand with my hot teaspoon. They'd jump. I'd giggle. A bit of joy was spread. On this day, though, I wasn't stirring a cup of tea. I'd poured boiling hot water into the teapot and was stirring that instead. The fact that this was going to make my spoon even hotter than normal escaped me and, when I glanced to my left and saw Mum concentrating on her sandwich making, my habit took over. My spoon came straight out of the teapot and went straight onto her lovely, delicate, pink neck. Not surprisingly, she jumped. I giggled. She told me what she thought of me and then we chuckled together.

That night, after tea, I took all the cups and saucers into the kitchen to wash them, while Mum went to the freezer to get a loaf out for Ben's sandwiches the next day. As I stood at the sink, washing away, Mum came in behind me with the frozen loaf in her hand. She saw me with my back to her and the temptation proved too much. She swung the loaf – slam! – straight into the back of my neck!

I staggered, slumped and grabbed hold of the worktop to stop myself from falling completely. Although my head was spinning, I forced myself to turn round.

Mum was grinning. 'Oh, look at you!' She said. 'A big, tough guy, but you can't even take being hit by a loaf of bread!'

I said, 'Mum, it's frozen solid! It's the same as being hit by a brick!'

Her grin disappeared. She considered for a second, nodded, and said, 'Oh well. It was a hot spoon!'

And our chuckling began again.

Another time I was in the kitchen when Mum was spreading jam onto slices of bread. She passed me one and, rather than put it on the plate, I just held it in my hand as if I were thinking of throwing it at her – which, to be fair, is exactly what I was thinking of doing. Mum saw the look in my eyes, realised what was in my mind, and gave me a look back that said, 'Oh yeah! You wouldn't dare!' As she did so, however, she was spreading jam as fast as she could onto her own slice of bread. We watched each other, both of us grinning, daring the other one to make the first move. It was like a scene from High Noon, but with jam. Suddenly, Mum turned to face me. I responded in kind and – splat! – we both got a jam sandwich in the face. Then, as we always did, we rolled up laughing.

Mum didn't ask me too much about my reasons for coming home, which was just as well. Things had been getting nasty at the JKA ever since Enoeda Sensei had returned to England the previous summer. Mick Dewey and Bob Waterhouse had stayed on in Japan for six or seven weeks before eventually leaving and, with the South Africans gone, it was back down to just Ray and me. Once again we were the only foreigners at the JKA.

There was some political crap going on, and a couple of the instructors were being real arseholes. What is also true is that, at that time, I probably wasn't the most pleasant person to be around. I was still training six hours a day, five days a week, on virtually no food. While my karate had really improved, and I could definitely fight, everything was beginning to feel far too personal. The result was that, when one particular instructor got personal with me, I felt obliged to get personal back. To cut the story down quite a bit, I left the JKA having given this instructor my opinion! It wasn't as if I left under a cloud, but I certainly didn't leave feeling happy.

I hadn't been back long when Enoeda Sensei's secretary called to say that he wanted to see both Ray and me. We met in the pub near the *dojo*. I could see from Sensei's face that we weren't meeting for a cuddle and a welcome home, and I felt my heartbeat quicken.

I was still struggling to come down from the daily adrenaline rush I'd experienced for over a year in Japan. Living a normal life back in England was taking some getting used to – it was harder than I'd ever imagined it would be – and the last thing I needed now was a telling-off from the man who had been, and still was, my inspiration.

Ray started to make polite conversation. Sensei just stared at me and I stared right back at him. He'd never looked at me like this before, nor I at him. Finally, he said, 'What happened in Japan?'

I knew what he was talking about, and I was equally sure he knew the answer to his question. Perhaps, in hindsight, I could have managed our meeting differently, but right then I was feeling angry and hurt. Surely he, of all people, understood what I'd been through?

I just said, 'What do you mean, "What happened?" '

He said, 'Did you have a problem before you left?'

I nodded. 'Yes.'

'That instructor had had some bad experiences abroad,' Sensei said.

'That's no excuse for treating people badly,' I replied, feeling my blood pounding.

Sensei pointed his finger at me. He managed to say only, 'You have to understand—' when I lost it completely.

I slapped his hand away, saying, 'I don't take that from anyone any more. Not even you!'

Whoom! He was on his feet in a flash!

Whoom! So was I!

Now we'd both reached the point of no return.

He pointed his finger again. 'You, finished!' he said. 'In KUGB, finished! In England, finished! You are nothing! Get out!'

I said, 'Right! I'll be outside! I'll wait there, then I'll go home!' And I stormed out.

By the time I was outside I'd realised the absurdity of what I'd just said. I counted, one, two, three, four, five, very quickly and I was off! I wasn't going to count slowly in case Sensei did follow me out. Mind you, if he had, he wouldn't have done anything. He was above that.

Ray phoned me a bit later and said, 'You mad, mad bastard! What were you thinking of?'

Looking back on it, I think I was fucked in the head. After a year of intense training and fighting with the best *karateka* on the planet, I think I was a bit like the soldier returning home from war who doesn't realise what's happened to his mind.

Whatever the reason, that was the start of my exile from Sensei, the time when some people referred to me as Ronin – a masterless samurai. It was to last eighteen months, during which time I was to have many experiences and learn many things.

Chapter 32

A HELPING HAND

Most important of all, my exile from Sensei became a time of consolidation. I trained on my own a lot, but now I was not under duress and I was eating good, regular food. I was able to evaluate my skill and, away from the pressures of the JKA, review what I had learned in Japan. In hindsight, I think that if I'd gone straight back into the *dojo* with Sensei I'd have just fallen into line and perhaps not analysed my karate as much as I did.

Invitations to teach also started to roll in. I taught for Kawazoe Sensei at Philbeach gardens, the *dojo* that Enoeda Sensei and I had started, and at a few different clubs around the country. It was then that a guy called Cliff Hepburn offered to help me out. Cliff organised a lot of karate competitions in those days. He was a good administrator and had a large network of contacts. He invited me to Manchester to do a demo at the European

Championships and, while I was there, he said, 'There's a lot of people who know you're back, and they would have you at their *dojo* if they knew how to contact you.'

I said, 'I don't know what to do about it.'

Cliff immediately offered to organise things for me – for a percentage, obviously. We agreed a contract and he did a great job getting me bookings. Without Cliff, I don't know if I would have done as well professionally as I have. He was precisely the helping hand that I needed!

One of the things I had to get used to, especially in the early days of being a professional instructor, was having to show people what I could do. When I first arrived at a new *dojo*, it was more like a proving ground than a teaching environment. Once I'd proved what I was capable of – or, at least, proved that I was far more capable than they were – I could get on and do some teaching. Quite often, that meant I had to spar with the senior black belts before I could really teach them anything. That was fine by me! If I needed to punch or kick a few people before they'd accept my level of skill, I was more than willing to oblige. I'd spent a year sparring with Yahara Sensei on an almost daily basis, so there was no way anyone here was going to test me. It was fun, though.

The first time I went to the Sendai *dojo* in Sunderland I realised that I was in precisely that type of situation. Some sparring was called for and I was happy to answer the call. Sendai was the biggest club in England at the time. I'd been invited there by one of the instructors, Owen Murray, a very tough guy and an excellent *karateka*, who had lost his left hand in an accident. We were to become good friends, but on this first visit he and the other *dan* grades just wanted to see what I was made of.

The first class was in the basement of the local YMCA. The only students present were the senior instructors and a few other hard types. They wanted to know what I could do and they were certainly up for it. It was clear from the start that these guys weren't interested in posturing or posing, they just wanted to know if I could use what I was demonstrating. So I sparred with them all and answered their questions. By the end of the class they were very happy.

It was the start of a very good relationship and I became a regular visitor to that part of the world. There are a lot of good people up there, with no edge to them at all, and I've always enjoyed my time among them. It was in Sunderland that I first met Jeff Westgarth, who is a giant of a man, not just in stature but as a man. He continues to run a fantastic karate group, and I'm honoured to teach them.

A few years after our first meeting, Owen came down to Brighton with a group of his black belts to train with me for a few days. My Brighton *dojo* had a very strong reputation and attracted a lot of very good people. In-between training, Owen asked if we could go on a trip to the East End. He'd never been and was keen to have a look round, so I took him and his boys down the Roman Road to a little pub that I knew.

It was the sort of place that had a little window in the door, with a slide across it, so the doorman could look out and see who was knocking. If he knew who you were, he let you in. If he didn't, the door remained closed. Once inside, we walked up to the bar and exchanged pleasantries with the owner, an ex-boxer, as he sorted our drinks. As we were talking, the owner noticed the glove on Owen's false hand.

'What have you done to your hand, son?' he asked.

To which Owen promptly grinned and took it off.

'I'm sorry, son,' the owner said.

'That's all right,' Owen replied, putting his hand back on. 'I lost it ages ago.'

Now, you've got to picture this little pub – small groups of men, sitting at tables, doing their deals, minding their own business. At one table, there was a larger group engaged in what looked like a very serious conversation. No one was taking any notice of us.

Owen began talking about karate to the governor of the pub. He got so caught up in it that he demonstrated a back fist with his false hand. But he hadn't fastened it back on properly. The hand flew across the room and hit one of the guys in the large group on the back of his head. They all leaped to their feet and, the next minute, we'd got three guns pointing at us! We all put our hands up instinctively, and you can imagine how these guys stared when they saw Owen with both arms in the air but only one hand!

'I'm sorry mate,' Owen said. 'My hand just flew off.'

It was all very serious for a few seconds, then the place was in uproar. It cost us a few drinks to get Owen's hand back, but at least he didn't get filled with lead.

There was a time when someone didn't return Owen's hand. It was when he was working the doors in Sunderland. He'd given a guy a little clump and thrown him out. As the guy walked away, he'd got a bit cheeky and Owen had taken his hand off and thrown it at him. It was a good shot, hitting the fella in the middle of his back. He promptly did no more than pick up Owen's hand and run off with it! The funny thing was that Owen was at a wedding a couple of days later, and the only spare hand he'd got at home was a right one. Owen, being Owen, put that on anyway, and went to the wedding with two right hands. Still, at least he'd have been able to shake hands with two people at once!

Chapter 33

A GOAT IN TURKEY

I was invited to teach in Turkey by a guy called Alev Oral, who'd trained with me at Philbeach Gardens. In the end I went over several times and, once we'd all got to know each other, I was treated very well.

My third trip marked the opening of a beautiful new *dojo*. The plan was that I'd teach for a week, then the *dojo* would be opened officially and I'd run a weekend course. The opening was to be a big, formal affair, with the mayor and local dignitaries attending and lots of press coverage. I'd been asked to cut the ribbon along with the mayor, and then do a demo using some of the black belts from the club.

The thing I liked most about the *dojo* was the fact that it had its own mascot, a young goat, who lived outside. At first I was surprised to see him there, but the local instructors explained that the new *dojo* was of such importance it needed a mascot.

When I heard that I thought, What a lovely idea!

Every morning, I kept some of my breakfast and fed it to the goat before the first class began. We became such good mates that I even gave him a name, Paddy, after Paddy McGinty's goat.

The week's training was good, Paddy put on a bit of weight and life was wonderful. We practised our demonstration – all the usual stuff, with me defending myself against four of the instructors – and made the final preparations for the big day.

It all went really well. Or, rather, it all went really well at first...

All the guests arrived as planned. I, of course, was early. The mayor and me cut the ribbon. That earned us a huge round of applause – which was only right, because it is a tricky job. The photographers took photos. The speechmakers made speeches. The people who didn't have either a camera to point or a speech to make clapped at every available opportunity.

Then, to make things even better, one of the instructors brought Paddy round and we all posed for photos with him.

Then, to make things as bad as they could possibly be, the instructor pulled out a blade that would have frightened the Devil, grabbed Paddy by his ears, pulled his head back and cut his throat!

The photographers took photos. Somebody made a speech. Everyone else clapped.

Everyone apart from me and Paddy. I was in shock and he was twitching and shaking on the ground. I couldn't believe what had happened and I screamed abuse. Some people – those whose English wasn't that good – thought

I was making a speech. Which was an easy mistake to make. After all I wasn't clapping and I didn't have a camera. The instructor, however, realised that I wasn't too happy.

He took me to one side and explained that killing a goat at an event like this was a local custom, and that all of the meat would be given to the poorest people in the area. I think that was supposed to calm me down, but it didn't. Hell, this wasn't a lump of meat on the ground! This was my mate Paddy!

My revenge was swift and decisive.

I had no choice but to go ahead with the demonstration. I was able, though, to make a few alterations to the planned moves. The demo was scheduled to last for nearly ten minutes. It actually lasted about thirty seconds. The four instructors attacked me in the ways we'd rehearsed, and I battered them all in ways that we hadn't!

When they were finally able to get to their feet and bow, the mayor led the applause. He was, it seems, mightily impressed by the realism of my work and the acting skills of my opponents. They, on the other hand, had just realised that you don't hurt any of my friends – let alone cut their throat!

Chapter 34

THAT'S ENTERTAINMENT!

I've always enjoyed cars and I've owned a large variety of them. At one time I had a Ford Sierra 2x2. It was gunmetal grey with a dark red stripe down the side, very classy looking and very nifty. It was just my type of car, very tight, very lean. I loved it.

One night I drove to Orpington to teach a class, and I parked it in a massive car park. In I went, did the business, and came out a couple of hours later with my bag over my shoulder and not a care in the world. It was then that I saw him. The car thief. He was standing by my car, with a set of keys in his hand, trying to find one that would open the driver's door. He was obviously wary and kept glancing around to make sure that no one had spotted what he was up to. I realised that, if I was going to have any chance of getting up close and personal, I'd have to walk across the car park as if I still didn't have a care in the world. Care in the world? If I'd been a couple of minutes later I wouldn't have had a car in the world!

I began to walk in his direction, looking beyond him to suggest that my car was parked somewhere else. Have you ever thought about what you'd do if you caught someone breaking into your home or your car? If you have, have you told yourself, 'I'd have 'em!'? Well there he was, trying to steal my pride and joy, and I was definitely going to have him!

I kept walking. When he glanced at me, I looked away. I waited until I was only three car lengths away from him, then I dropped my bag and was on him like a wild cat. He went down in an instant. I rolled him out of the way, took my own car keys out of my pocket and tried to open the door. I couldn't! The prick had obviously damaged the lock. I had a couple more attempts. It was no use. Although I'd stopped him from stealing my car, I hadn't stopped him from damaging it! Damn! I should have hit him harder!

But then, as I looked round the car park, I saw another Sierra two rows away. It was identical to mine. The same model, the same gunmetal grey, the same red stripe, the same everything. Then I looked at the number plate of the car I was standing next to. This wasn't my car! My Sierra was the one parked two rows away. This Sierra belonged to the man on the floor. I'd just knocked out a guy for struggling to get into his own vehicle!

I rolled him onto his side, made sure that he was breathing OK, and drove away. It was only a few miles later that I began to consider how the guy could possibly explain his lumps and bumps when he got home. If he was married, what would he say to his wife to convince her that he was an innocent party?

'No, I wasn't mugged. No, I didn't start a fight! No, darling, I promise you it wasn't the husband of a woman I'm having an affair with! It was a complete stranger, I swear to you, who hit me for no reason at all and then ran off!'

The poor guy! I often wonder whether he got another clump when he got home.

On another occasion I was driving Kawazoe Sensei back to his home after training when we were cut up by this complete idiot. He did it once and I ignored him. Normally I would have flashed my lights or made a gesture just to register my displeasure, but that didn't seem the right thing to do with Kawazoe Sensei in the car. He is one of the best karate technicians in the world. He also has a very gentle disposition, and I didn't want to start effing and blinding or causing a row with him next to me.

Anyway, because I'd let the guy get away with it the first time, he decided to do it again. A few seconds later we pulled up at a set of lights just before my favourite building in London, the Natural History Museum. Dickhead pulled up next to me. He looked over to make sure that he'd got my attention and then he grinned.

I said to Kawazoe Sensei, 'Do you know what? If I was on my own I'd get out and give him a dig.'

He nodded and said, 'OK.'

I took that as a green light – which, to be fair, may not have been what he meant – and before the K had joined the O in his 'OK' I was out of the car and heading round the front of Dickhead's motor!

I glared in through the windscreen and saw the look on his face change. He realised that he was in trouble, that things were suddenly not going according to plan, and locked his driver's door just before I reached it. It didn't matter. He still wasn't as safe as he thought he was. I ignored the door and fired a roundhouse kick into his windscreen. I had no intention of breaking it, I just wanted to shock him and I did that all right!

'You!' I snarled. 'Get out of the fucking car!'

For some reason, he wasn't keen. I punched the door window. It smashed. Dickhead screamed. He put the car into gear and drove off, ignoring the red lights.

When I got back into my car, I apologised to Kawazoe Sensei.

'No problem,' he said. We drove in silence for a while, and then he decided to offer some feedback. 'The round-house kick was not so good,' he said. 'The punch was OK, though.'

When Ben wanted to buy a new car I was more than happy to help him. We found one that was he interested in and I drove him to Ilford, where the then owner lived. I didn't know the area and was going slowly to make sure I didn't miss the road I was looking for, when, all of a sudden, we were overtaken by a couple of guys in a Dormobile. They flashed their lights, made the usual rude gestures and called us all the names under the sun.

It was more than enough to make the red mist descend. However fast they were going, my temper was quicker. I thought to myself, No! I'm not having that! And I set off after them.

I drove past and cut them off, forcing them to stop. I ran round to the passenger door and slid it open.

'Who's fucking clever now, then?' I said, and clumped the guy nearest to me before either of them had chance to answer.

The driver held his hands up, saying, 'I'm sorry! I'm sorry! We were wrong in what we did and, to be fair, it wasn't him: it was me!'

Really? Now, I've always believed in being honest – even when it hurts – and this guy had been brutally honest. Well, actually he'd just been honest. I was going to be brutal!

I was round his side of the Dormobile in a flash. I grabbed him by his hair to pull him out, but he immediately looped his arms through the steering wheel to stop me. There we were, him holding on for dear life and me trying to get my knee in his face. The air was blue. I've got a terrible mouth on me when I lose my temper and I was certainly telling this guy what I thought of him.

Meanwhile, Ben had got out of our car and was checking on the passenger, who was slumped forward holding his head. When he was sure that the passenger was still in one piece, Ben came round to where I was – still swearing and belting the driver, doing my best to get him out – and said, 'That's enough, son. Come on.'

He led me away and we drove off. Neither of us felt like test-driving the car we had come to see, so we returned home. On the way, my temper subsided. I said, 'I'm sorry about that, Ben.'

'That's all right, son,' he said. 'But you didn't have to use such bad language!'

He didn't mention the incident again until we got home, and then, as he got out of the car, he looked back and said quietly, 'Thanks for the entertainment, son.'

Chapter 35

DRINK

I believe some people are genetically programmed to be alcoholics. I believe I'm one of them. I don't know whether the many little tipples I had as a child in my grandparents' pub had much influence. I do know that, as a teenager, I hardly drank. When I began training in karate – in the years before I went to Japan – I drank even less. I had the occasional lager at parties and at special times, such as Christmas, but apart from that I'd sip an orange juice. I was very clean-living and very healthy.

It was when I returned from Japan in 1978 that I started drinking seriously. I began boozing with lads from the East End and found that I had an incredible tolerance for alcohol. I could drink as much as any of the hardened drinkers I knew without ever getting a hangover. By then I'd finished my career as a karate competitor and was beginning to make a living for myself as an instructor.

Every weekend I travelled to teach a course and every weekend my hosts took me out for a meal and drinks. Lots of drinks. Everyone wanted to say thank you by buying me a drink. And I, being sociable, always said yes.

What you have to understand is that for these people this was a special event. They got drunk like that only whenever they invited me to do a course, which was two or three times a year. For me, it was happening every weekend. It wasn't long before I found myself looking forward to the socialising as much as the teaching.

As I developed as a drinker, I began to realise that I was happier drinking alone, indoors, rather than in a pub or club. I'd worked in those places for so long that I knew there was always the chance of something kicking off. Whereas at home there'd be no trouble and, just as important, I wouldn't have to wait for a barman to serve me. It wasn't long before I'd come home, full of adrenaline, having taught karate all night, and need at least half a bottle of vodka before I could go to sleep. That soon turned into a full bottle. I'd have to sit up until 3 a.m. drinking and watching TV. I couldn't relax until I'd had enough alcohol.

The strange thing was that no matter how much I drank, or whatever time I went to bed, I was always able to get up at 7 a.m. and go training. I've discovered since that many alcoholics are successful professionals. It's a mistake to think that alcoholics are always jobless, penniless and living in the gutter. Some of the most addicted drinkers on the planet are senior bankers, business people and lawyers. You can be a drunk and still be a top-class professional. I know. I am one. And that adds to the problem because people see you being good at your job and say, 'Don't worry, you're not an alcoholic, you're just a heavy drinker.' Wrong! Fucking wrong, wrong, wrong!

With women, everything was great when we first met. After all, I was 'good-time' Dave, who travelled around the world teaching karate. The other thing that helped is that I'm a nice drunk. Give me enough alcohol and I just giggle, cuddle and fall asleep in a corner. The truth is, I'm far more spiteful when I'm sober. It was only when a relationship developed to the point where the woman moved in with me and saw the extent of my drinking that the problems started. Then she'd realise that I was 'good-time' Dave who spent half his life in the dojo and the other half in a bottle of vodka.

No one in their right mind wants to share that with you.

Chapter 36

'I'LL END UP ON DEATH ROW AND YOU'LL FLY HOME TO YOUR PALACE'

One of my regulars in the barber's shop was a lovely guy known as Ray the Chat, or Ray the Talker. You can guess why he was called that, right? He just never shut up. I mean, people who know me think I can talk a lot, but I'm as quiet as a mouse compared with Ray the Chat.

Ray wasn't a fighter. He was a talker who wasn't scared of anyone. That's not a healthy combination and it got him into all sorts of bother. I can't tell you the number of times I watched Ray spend ten minutes talking himself into a fight and the next two hours talking himself out of it. Then he'd walk away with his chest puffed out, feeling good, looking as if he'd just won a victory. Meanwhile, the other guy would be standing there going, 'What the hell's just happened? I was gonna knock his block off for the first ten minutes, then I started to feel sorry for him, and now he's making out as if he's given me a good hiding!' Of course, Ray also liked to talk to the ladies, and as a result he'd got kids all over the place. I'm godfather to one of them.

You won't be surprised to know that Ray was a wheeler-dealer. You name it and Ray was involved in it. Every time you met him, he was doing something different. At one time he worked as a chauffeur for a high-ranking Arab prince who was staying in London. One day the inevitable happened and the prince told Ray that he'd got a bit of a problem, to which Ray, in his infinite wisdom, replied, 'I can have that sorted.'

Ray came to me and asked if I'd help out. I said, 'Of course, mate. As long as it's nothing too silly.'

'No, it's not,' Ray said. 'You've just got to have a word with someone.'

'Fair enough.'

Now, as I've said, I'm not a big bloke, which means that sometimes people don't take me too seriously if I'm only talking to them. They do tend to take me very seriously if we get past the talking stage, but Ray had assured me that wasn't needed in this particular situation. So I took a very lumpy mate along with me – just for the visual effect – had a few words and, sure enough, the problem went away.

I promptly forgot about it and carried on doing what I was doing. The prince left London and went to Texas. While he was there, he decided that he needed someone he could trust to look after his security and remembered me. The next thing you know, I got a phone call from Ray asking if I'd like to go over there, hire a new security team and take charge of it for him. We negotiated a nice little contract and I was off to Houston.

When I arrived, I was given a Cadillac, keys to a flat and a gun. The car and the flat were great, but I wasn't at all happy with the gun. I said, 'I'm sorry, but I don't use these. Besides, you haven't hired me to fire a gun. You can find plenty of people over here who could shoot my toes off, so I don't need to carry that.'

The prince replied, 'If you refuse, I'll have to send you back home on the next plane.'

'Look,' I said, 'that's fine for you, but I'm likely to shoot myself with it. Even worse, I might shoot someone else and then I'll end up on Death Row and you'll fly home to your palace.'

'I promise you, you won't have any problems like that,' he said. 'If you work for me you have diplomatic immunity.'

And I did. He gave me the card and everything. I realised later that all he really wanted me to do was just carry the gun around and, thankfully, I never put myself or anyone else at risk with it.

Now, I have to tell you the work of a bodyguard is not at all glamorous or exciting. Actually, the work is crap. I was on call twenty-four hours a day and worked at least sixteen of those hours. It was often very monotonous, and the challenge was to stay aware and alert at all times. If you let the boredom get to you or any of your team, the security could break down.

When you are working for someone as rich as the prince it becomes even more demanding, because he's used to doing anything he wants any time of the day or night. When you have that much money and you come from a powerful royal family, people will do whatever you ask them to. You can buy anything, and just about everyone is for sale. Talk about how the other half lives!

The prince would think nothing of playing back-gammon with his friends until two or three o'clock in the morning and then turning round to me and saying, 'Dave, I want to go shopping now. Organise it.'

I'd then be on the phone arranging for a shopping mall to open up just for him from 4 until 6 a.m. Of course, the manager of the mall would be delighted to do it, because he knew the prince was going to spend thousands of dollars. Which he always did. When we got to the mall, the prince would have three people following behind him pushing shopping trolleys, and he'd just walk round throwing things into them – jewellery, clothing, anything that took his fancy. To be fair, he'd always say, 'Dave, pick some things for yourself.'

That was one of the perks of the job and, in many ways, the prince was a nice guy. You have to remember, though, that money meant nothing to him. Ray and me worked it out that he earned more in one night while he slept than either of us did in years!

Organising trips for the prince meant that I had to do a lot more than simply get managers to open their stores, or book rooms in restaurants and nightclubs. I had total responsibility for his safety, so I had to plan routes and do a risk assessment of every place we visited. I had to decide the best way to get him into a building without attracting too much attention, and the best way to get him out in case of an emergency. I made the decisions about where to place the rest of the team and how we'd respond if certain problems occurred. To be honest, it was all common sense to me, based on knowledge I'd developed over a long period of time.

The funny thing about running a security team is that you're actually preparing for the very event you're planning to avoid. In other words, if you do your job right the odds are that there won't be any trouble. That doesn't mean it can't happen, though.

On one occasion, the prince decided that he wanted to go to a particular nightclub. I went there a couple of days before, met the manager, and told him that the prince and his entourage were planning to visit. I asked him what security the nightclub would have working that night. I explained which room we needed and which areas had to be cordoned off, and I checked out all the usual places – entrances and exits, toilets, even the roof. I had a team of fifteen people working with me and they were all good. I put some in the car park, some inside the building, a couple on the roof. I arrived with the prince, everything was going OK, when all of a sudden a fella in the car park pulled out a gun! It turned out that he was wanting to have a go at his mate, who had upset him, but within half a second he'd got my people all over him ready to blow his head off! I just covered the prince and got him out of the way. The prince was never in danger. The guy in the car park wasn't so lucky – he really had picked the wrong day to fall out with his friend!

A more serious worry for me was that the IRA was very active at that time, and there was some weird stuff going on, even in Houston. There was an Irish pub there and Ray and I popped in one day for a drink. Someone had put jars on the bar saying 'Contribute to the IRA', which I really didn't like. Anyway, I ordered a couple of beers and the bartender shook one of the jars and said, 'You can have a beer if you put something in this.' There was no chance of that! The IRA didn't get their contribution and I didn't get my beer.

Whenever I wasn't guarding the prince, I trained. I'd found the Black Belt Academy in Houston, run by a real character called Gary Lee, and I spent a lot of time there. I was what Gary called a 'fourth degree' black belt. I didn't tell him about my time at the JKA or being part of the England team. I just kept quiet and got on with my own training. I used the bags and the *makiwara* and, occasionally, joined in some of the classes. It was a great *dojo* and I learned a lot from Gary. Specifically, I learned how to market and promote a *dojo*. For the first time in my life I saw someone running a successful martial arts business. It was so far removed from anything I'd experienced in either Japan or the UK that it took me by complete surprise.

I remember the first time I watched Gary initiate someone into his *dojo*. In the UK you simply turned up, paid your £1 or whatever it was, and joined in. Not here! Once Gary had persuaded the newcomer to sign up to a direct-debit scheme, he sold him a karate suit. This, though, was only the beginning.

'Do you want your name embroidered on your suit?' Gary asked.

The guy clearly hadn't thought of this before. 'Erm, I'm not sure.'

Gary had no intention of being put off by something as trivial as a little hesitation. 'What?' he asked. 'Aren't you proud of your name?'

'Oh, yeah. Of course I am. Yeah, you're right! I'll have my name on it.'

'Good. And I guess you'll want the name of the *dojo* embroidered on the leg of your suit?'

'Erm...'

'You'd better be proud of the *dojo*.'

'Oh, yeah. Of course, yeah, I'll have that.'

By the time your first meeting with Gary was over you'd paid a fortune and you hadn't even had one lesson!

The students there were willing to sew the most amazing things onto their *gis*. One night I joined in a class and found myself sparring a young black belt. He came at me like a really angry young bull charging at a gate. The first couple of times I just palmed him away. By the third time I was getting pissed off, and I hit him hard in the back of his head with an *ushiro mawashi-geri* – a back roundhouse kick. The rest of the class was watching and everyone broke into applause.

'Mr Hazard,' Gary said, 'where did that kick come from?'

'I've always had it,' I told him.

'But Mr Hazard, we didn't know you could do that.'

'You never asked.'

The next day the young black belt arrived at the *dojo* with enough writing to fill a book sewn onto the back of his karate suit. Two of the sentences read, 'I must control my temper' and 'I must learn to recognise my place.' I'd have loved to have seen him walk into the JKA wearing that *gi*!

In the entrance hall to the academy there were loads of huge trophies – some of which were even bigger than me. Several of them proclaimed Gary as 'World Champion'.

When I first saw them I thought to myself, Christ! This guy must be good! Then I learned that, in the US, you could get a trophy just for competing, and another one if you got through to the last eight. If you won a competition you could go home with three or sometimes four trophies! As for being World Champion, as Gary explained it, 'Some of the competitions are quite small, but they are open to anyone in the world who wants to enter.'

That said, I don't want to take anything away from Gary. He was absolutely fearless and would have fought anyone. In fact, when he did demonstrations he'd often invite people from the audience to get in the ring and spar a round with him. The first time he invited me to take part in a demonstration with him, I wasn't aware of this custom, and it almost got us shot!

Gary had agreed to do a demo at what was called a 'shitkicker's club'. This was a cowboys' drinking club. The night's entertainment was going to begin with some boxing, followed by Gary sparring two of his students. Then I would do a traditional *kata* and, finally, two girls with big tits would mud-wrestle. Not surprisingly, the cowboys were not that interested in what I'd got to show them. Once I'd finished, I went straight back to the changing room. It was while I was there that Gary made his usual offer to the audience.

'If any of you guys want to spar a round when we come back after the break, just let me know.'

Then he joined me in the changing room. The next minute this huge Texan lump charges in saying, 'Right! Who is it I've got to fight?'

He, of course, was talking about in the ring, with the gloves on, after the break. I, of course, thought he wanted a scrap.

'Try me!' I said and knocked him unconscious.

Suddenly, Gary was shouting his head off. 'Mr Hazard! Mr Hazard! What did you do that for?'

'Because he wanted to fight one of us,' I said. 'And, as I was closest to him, I thought I'd sort it.'

'But Mr Hazard, I told people to come backstage and let me know if they wanted to spar a round.'

'Oops!'

What made it worse was the fact that this guy had got three equally large friends, all with guns on their hips, waiting for him at the bar. They were very unhappy about what I'd done. It cost me all the money I'd been paid for doing the demo, plus more besides, to buy them beers for the rest of the night.

Chapter 37

THE ONLY WOMAN MORE BEAUTIFUL THAN A PRIMA BALLERINA IS A PRIMA BALLERINA WITH BOOBS!

The prince decided that he wanted to go the ballet, so I went ahead and checked out the usual stuff. The royal box was fine and I made all the necessary arrangements. The performance started. I was standing near him making sure that he was safe and his entourage were happy, when this beautiful woman appeared on stage. I mean, she was really beautiful! All of a sudden three things were happening at once. I was guarding a prince, she was on the stage bouncing around as the star of the show, and I was falling in love. She not only moved like a dream and had the body of a professional dancer, but she'd got boobs! I'd never seen a ballerina with a body like that before. They all train so hard that normally everything falls off.

That night, as I watched her dance, I learned something really important, and I'll tell you what it was – the only woman more beautiful than a prima ballerina is a prima ballerina with boobs!

I began thinking to myself, I have to meet this woman!

So I said to the prince, 'Wouldn't it be really nice if you met the cast and we bought them some flowers?'

'That's a good idea,' he said.

That gave me until the end of the performance to sort it all out. I said to Ray, 'I want loads of flowers for the cast here by the time they finish.'

He wasn't sure why, but recognised the look on my face and got on with it.

I visited the stage manager and said, 'Look, I've got this very important and very rich prince upstairs who would like to meet the cast.'

He wasn't convinced, shaking his head, saying, 'Oh, I dunno. I don't think that's possible.

I said, 'Listen! This man is worth an absolute fortune. Wouldn't it be nice if he sponsored you for the next year or two?'

Suddenly he realised that everything was possible. 'Yes, of course,' he said. 'He can meet all the cast as soon as he wants.'

I went back to the prince and told him that the cast would love to meet him. He was delighted.

After the show, we went backstage. The cast were all lined up. I introduced the prince to the stage manager and he took us down the line. As soon as the prince had been introduced to the beautiful ballerina and had moved on to the next dancers, I went back to her and said, 'Excuse me, the prince would love to invite you and a friend and your husbands or boyfriends to dinner tomorrow night. Would you be able to come?'

She said she'd love to, and I told her to arrive at a top restaurant at a certain time.

I didn't say a word to the prince. Instead, I booked a couple of tables and arrived in the restaurant ahead of time with Ray the Chat. The plan was that if Deborah and her friend turned up with two men we'd say that the prince had been unavoidably detained and we'd leave them to it. If they turned up on their own, we'd say that the prince regretted he couldn't come but had insisted that we sit at the next table to ensure their safety. During the course of the meal we'd then do our best to join them.

Sure enough, Deborah and her friend arrived without company. They accepted the prince's apologies and found us impossible to ignore. Deborah asked us to join them and by the end of the evening the job was done.

Some time later the prince had to return to Saudi Arabia sooner than expected, which meant cutting my contract short. He more than honoured it, though. He gave me all the money I was due, and he left me with the keys to the Cadillac. Suddenly, I had the chance to live like royalty myself. My time was all my own again and, after so many long, boring days guarding the prince, I was desperate to have some fun. I was, by my standards, wealthy – although the money didn't last for long. I had a fabulous place to live and a great car to drive around in. On top of that, I had the beautiful Deborah. If I was going to live like a king for a couple of months, she was going to be my queen.

Deborah and I had a fabulous time in America. We loved each other's company and had some great experiences together. I had plenty of money in my pocket, a fine car and a penthouse to live in. Then we moved back to England, to the East End, where my prima ballerina swapped a penthouse fit for a prince for 'the Little House on the Hairy'.

We married pretty quickly because we wanted to and because Deborah needed a visa. It was the best wedding I've ever been to. I'm not saying that because it was mine. It's just true. I told the family that I didn't want any fuss and I invited only a few, close mates. One of them, Johnny Farley, arranged a pub for the reception and the landlord lent us his Rolls-Royce. My family were up the night before doing the food, while Deborah slept at Johnny's place with his girlfriend and he stayed with me.

The next day we were married at Leyton Register Office. Deborah looked beautiful. The photographer we hired was a cracker. He managed to take one photo of Deborah and me standing together, smiling outside the register office, with a bloody great 'No entry' sign right behind us!

In the pub, I put £300 behind the bar to buy everyone their first drink and then we had a proper East End get-together. And that was that. I was married on a bootlace and we all had a lovely time.

The only person who didn't enjoy it as much as everyone else was my lovely, protective sister, Janice. She actually came round before the wedding with a bottle in her hand and said, 'Do you want to call it off and go for a drink?' Obviously I didn't but, looking back on it, I realise Janice was right.

While I was at home in the streets of the East End, my prima ballerina wasn't. It was a very different lifestyle from what she had been used to. One night, for example, after training and dinner, we were driving home about midnight when I got into a bit of a conflict with another driver. I was driving a left-hand-drive Granada at the time and I must have accidentally cut up a guy in a Mini. Anyway, at the next set of lights he pulled up to me and called me a wanker!

I said to him, 'If you want to make something out of it, just pull over!'

The guy did, so I told Deborah to lock all the doors and to drive away if things turned out wrong. As I was in a left-hand-drive car I was out, on the pavement, and ready to go before the other guy had even opened his door.

He was huge! He just kept uncoiling out of this tiny Mini!

I thought, I'm not giving him a chance, and I was on him in a flash, knocking him out. At that moment a man in a suit came rushing up, waving his brolly, going, 'I saw it! I saw what happened!'

I said, 'Good! You saw him cut me up?'

He said, 'No! I just saw you punch him for no reason.'

I said, 'In that case, you're about to see me punch someone else.' And I knocked him out, too. As he fell to the pavement I saw a big blue light behind him. I was knocking people out right outside Holborn police station! Inside I could see two coppers staring out of the window, their mouths gaping open. One had his sandwich halfway up to his mouth and the other had a mug of tea in his hand. I thought, I'm bound to get arrested for this. And so I jumped back into the Granada. I asked Deborah if she'd seen where we were. She said, 'Do you mean outside a precinct? Sure I did.'

I spent three days waiting for the police to visit me, but

they never did. I also checked out the big guy I'd punched. He was a nightclub doorman, and I did visit him just to make sure that he didn't want to pursue it. He'd also found out who I was and he agreed to let it go.

Another time, at a party at the house of Harry Robinson (one of Dave Robinson's brothers), a guy started hassling Deborah. She was such a good-looking woman that men's eyes were always on her, but this guy pushed his luck. I was talking to some people in the lounge when she came out of the kitchen, where she'd been chatting to Dave and his brothers, and stood next to me. The bloke followed her in. I smiled at him and he said to Deborah, 'What I like about this guy is that every time I see him he's always smiling.'

Deborah said, 'Yeah, he's got lots of smiles and they mean lots of different things. This one means he'll smack your face in if you get too near his wife.'

The man just smirked and looked at me and said, 'Is that right?'

I smiled again – the same smile. 'Yeah.'

At which point Dave Robinson came over and said to the bloke, 'Do yourself a favour and fuck off!'

The man went home and we enjoyed the rest of the party.

Deborah and me were married for only four months, from September to January. Things came to a head on New Year's Eve, when her sister and a friend came over from America. We had a great party in 'the Little House on the Hairy', just me, two of my karate students – Mick Shea and Frank Gianotte – and the three girls. We were dancing and drinking for hours, having a lovely time. I even demonstrated my singing abilities, using a banana as a microphone.

Afterwards, when we were clearing up, Deborah accused me of dancing too much with her sister. Now, to me, you're dancing with a woman only if you're touching her, and I hadn't laid a hand on Deborah's sister, so I said, 'The only woman I danced with was you.'

Deborah wouldn't listen and became really angry. She had a glass in her hand and, as she walked past me to go out of the lounge, she swung it at my face. I was sure she'd cut me because I felt liquid on my cheek (which turned out to be booze, not blood) and my hands just moved instinctively to knock her arm away. In those days I used to wear a gold ring with my initials on and I accidentally caught Deborah with it and cut her eyebrow. It was a rotten, rotten feeling! It was the one time when my instinct was bad and, to this day, I've never worn a ring again. When I told Mick and Frank the next morning, they couldn't believe it. How could such a lovely party end like that?

Anyway, as far as Deborah and me were concerned, that was that. Our marriage was over and she decided to return to America. I paid for her ticket, and drove her to the airport. She got on the plane and I went back to the East End. In hindsight, it was the best thing for both of us – but I'll never forget the first time I saw her dancing on that stage!

Chapter 38

A TOBY IN BERKELEY SQUARE

Alan Dalton and Nick Parker ran markets around the edge of London in places such as Slough and Aldershot. I worked for them as the 'Toby' – which means the rent collector. The traders would arrive early in the morning and put their stalls up and I'd go round mid-afternoon, when they'd made a few quid, and ask for their rent for the day. Most of the time the regulars would just pay up. They were usually decent people and, besides that, they knew that if you were the Toby of a market you could handle yourself. It was a necessary skill, because every once in a while you'd have to deal with an arsehole.

Alan and Nicky wouldn't let in more than two people selling the same thing, whether it was shoes, jeans or whatever, and I made sure that competing traders didn't encroach on each other's patch. I very rarely had to get nasty with people, although occasionally we'd get travellers in and they could fuck it up a bit.

Once a traveller parked where he wasn't allowed to and made it clear that he wasn't going to behave. He was the kingpin of the local area and clearly fancied himself. Push came to shove and he told me that he wanted to have a go.

I said, 'Fair enough' and gave him a slap.

All of a sudden he was backing off with his hands in the air going, 'Hold up! Hold up! I'm not a well man!'

I said, 'You were well enough to want to take a shot at me.'

That observation didn't serve to calm him down. In fact, it did the opposite. The next minute he was telling me that he was going to come back and shoot me! I do take such threats personally – which is how I feel they're always meant – so I clumped him properly and threw him in the back of his car. When he came round he drove off, smashing the gate as he went. I did get a face to come down to the market for a time as a precaution, but the guy never came back.

One of the things I've learned over the years is that people who make a lot of noise threatening you usually do nothing. It's the quiet ones you have to be aware of.

It was Alan Dalton who introduced me to Morton's nightclub in Berkeley Square. It was a posh nightclub where many people would meet before going on to somewhere else. It had a bar, a tiny disco downstairs and a fantastic restaurant upstairs which, among other things, served a fabulous breakfast. It was always full of showbiz faces and I was to meet quite a few of them during my increasingly frequent visits. When Alan first took me there the guy behind the ramp – the bar – recognised me as one of Enoeda Sensei's students. He also studied karate and, to cut a long story short, by the end of the night I'd been given a life membership. This usually took months to arrange but, as with so many things, it's who you know and not what you know that counts.

As I've already said, I became a regular visitor. I'd often take Mick and Frank with me and I had many wonderful nights there, enjoying a few drinks some great food, watching the stars come in and out.

One night I was in Morton's when the lead singer of a very popular band came up to my table. He said, 'You're Dave Hazard, aren't you?' He didn't wait for a reply. He just went on, 'Do you know how much money you've cost me because my guitarist can't play?'

The background to this little incident was very simple. One of my karate students was a professional guitarist who happened to play in this gentleman's band. Unfortunately, the guitarist had broken some fingers while training and, although I heard that this singer believed in miracles, the guitarist didn't get one and was unable to go on tour. That meant, presumably, that a replacement had to be found and paid for.

I explained to this gentleman that doing karate was an individual's choice that brought with it certain risks. Although I appreciated the inconvenience it had caused, the accident wasn't really anything to do with me. He didn't see the sense in what I was saying and became quite rude. So, when he decided to stop being arsy with me and go to the gents', I decided to follow him. Once we were alone I was able to explain my point more clearly and, although our relationship didn't start with a kiss or end with one, we did come to a very definite, mutual agreement.

Some time later I was enjoying an afternoon session there when I became aware of Terry Venables, Alan Mullery and Malcolm Allison, all famous football managers, sitting at the bar. Mullery and Allison started having a bit of a to-do together and, a few seconds later, they were rolling around on the floor. Venables had nothing to do with it. He just sat at the bar, laughing. The doorman, a huge black guy, heard the schmozzle and came in to see what was going on, and I realised that he had a problem. He was obviously capable of pulling them apart, but if he hit either one of them he was probably going to get sacked. On the other hand, he couldn't afford to leave them alone. I thought I ought to lend him a hand, so I went across, pulled them apart, and told them to behave. They went back to the bar and became best of friends again. When I left, the doorman thanked me for helping him out.

On another occasion I had the privilege of meeting one of the world's top film stars. I'd reserved my table for 8.30 and, when I arrived with a couple of friends, a man was sitting in my seat entertaining some people. I told the fella working the ramp that I wanted my table. He said, 'They'll be gone in a minute, Mr Hazard.'

I said, 'I want them gone now!' I didn't know who was in my seat and I didn't care.

As it turned out, I didn't have to push the matter any further. The man came over and apologised for making us wait. He bought us a bottle of very nice wine and then politely excused himself. I can tell you now that Dustin

Hoffman is not only a great actor, he's a true gentleman – and the way he handled himself during our brief exchange was both impressive and a lesson to all those who think they are more important than they really are.

There were quite a lot of people going into Morton's around that time who thought they were the dog's bollocks – better than everyone else. I'd been taught by my Mum that no one was either better or worse than anyone else and we should treat everyone the same. So, even though I was training lots with the man who I thought was the best fighter in the world, it didn't make me superior to anyone else. How you carry yourself matters and – hey – remember, when it comes to a fight we've all only got one chance.

Chapter 39

THE MAN WITH HOGFEVER

I first met Richard La Plante, a man who carries himself very well, at the Budokwai in Kensington in 1981. I was teaching there occasionally and Caesar Andrews, one of the regular instructors, told me of a guy who wanted to take some private lessons with me. He explained that it was an American who was training at Enoeda Sensei's *dojo*. The guy was preparing for his third dan exam, which he planned to take in America under his original Sensei, Okazaki. While I was impressed with the man's etiquette – I thought it was quite appropriate that he should take such a senior grading under his own Sensei, even if it meant travelling halfway around the world – I still said no.

I didn't do private lessons in those days, so my message was, 'If you want to train with me, join the class like everyone else. You'll get enough out of that.'

Anyway, Mr La Plante received, but refused to accept,

my message and, after some pestering, I finally agreed to give him a private lesson.

We met at the Budokwai. He was a well-built, handsome guy, with a voice that reminded me of Harrison Ford. I said to him, 'What do you want to cover in this class?'

To my astonishment he replied, 'Can we do some sparring?'

This was a serious breach of etiquette. In Japan you never, ever, asked one of the instructors to spar. If you had it would have been taken as a challenge and the results would not have been pretty. An instructor could ask a junior to spar with him and then, usually, it was a fairly measured affair, with the junior being given the opportunity to learn something useful – albeit in a painful manner. But to do it the other way round was unthinkable! I couldn't imagine what would have happened if I'd asked Enoeda Sensei to spar with me. Actually, I could! I could imagine it all too clearly, and that, apart from the fact that I'd never have been deliberately rude to him, was enough to stop me from even thinking about it. If you asked an instructor to spar, you were considered to be asking him to fight – and Mr La Plante had just asked me to spar.

I said, 'Fair enough,' bowed immediately and got stuck in.

Even back then, Richard was a very capable *karateka*. He was also a decent grappler and a boxing coach. So I started out just seeing what he'd got, and then gearing it up until he couldn't take any more. We went at it for five minutes or so. By then it was clear that he couldn't cope. I bowed and ended the lesson. He went home with some lumps, bruises and a few strategically placed bite marks. I went out of the *dojo* with some of his blond hair in my hands. I didn't expect to see him again.

Imagine my surprise, then, when, a couple of days later, he called and asked for another lesson. I agreed, thinking that this time he'd want to do something that would be of more benefit. How wrong could I be? I asked him what he want to do and, again, he asked to spar. I went at him harder this time than I had in our first encounter. The lesson was even shorter and, when he left, I knew I'd seen the last of him.

No! A few days later he phoned again and arranged a third class. This time he asked if we could practise *kata*. I said, 'Today you may learn something. Why did you ask to spar before?'

He replied, 'I'd heard that you liked to spar and in a boxing gym people just get in the ring and work together. It doesn't mean anything.'

That made sense of what had happened. I'd never felt that there was anything spiteful about Richard. If I had I'd have dealt with him more severely. In fact, Richard is the opposite of spiteful. He's one of those people who are very easy to get along with. We quickly became friends and, to this day, he remains one of my favourite people.

Anyway, I gave him a series of lessons and he went back to Philadelphia, where he passed his third dan exam. He returned with a karate book for me signed by Okazaki Sensei, thanking me for my help.

Richard's soon-to-be-very-famous wife, the author and screenwriter Lynda La Plante, didn't think too much of me at first. Mind you, her husband was going home with hair missing and an assortment of lumps and bumps courtesy of yours truly.

The more I got to know Richard, the more I came to appreciate the fascinating and varied life that he led. At that time, he was selling high-class properties while working on his first novel, a martial arts fantasy called *Tegne*. He had also been in a rock band, walked barefoot across a Mexican desert and worked as a psychiatric counsellor. He based many of the characters in his novel on people he knew within the martial arts world. In the world of *Tegne* I became his fictional half-brother. In the real world I was just enjoying being friends with this brilliant, entertaining man.

Over the years I've learned a lot from Richard. He is a very worldly man who is always willing to explore other martial arts. Nowadays he lives about ten miles outside of Los Angeles, where he works as a novelist and screenwriter. He's also written a very well-known book about Harley-Davidson motorbikes, called *Hogfever*, and I'm in it. Richard's always had a thing about Harleys. He's got a fantastic eye for design and redesigns his own bikes.

We still keep in touch on a regular basis and meet whenever we can. He doesn't challenge me to spar any more though, which means that I can let his hair fall out naturally.

Chapter 40

DON'T MISTAKE POLITENESS FOR WEAKNESS

My sisters and me helped move Mum and Ben into a place in Walthamstow. It was a lovely house. The only problem was that a complete arsehole lived next door. He was the kind of guy who didn't show any respect to his neighbours, day or night. If he'd been living next door to me, it would have been dealt with very quickly without any consideration for the consequences. But he wasn't living next door to me, he was living next door to my parents, so things had to be done nicely.

I knew that Ben had been round a couple of times to have a word with him, but the guy had taken no notice. Whenever I saw him I'd tried to smile and be nice, but he wasn't having any of it. Mum didn't say too much to me about the situation, because she didn't want me involved. Eventually, though, it reached a point where it had to be sorted.

I went round and knocked him up. I said, 'Do you mind being a bit more quiet? You're really disturbing my parents. The other thing is, your guttering needs fixing and it's leaking onto their house. I'll pay for that myself, if you just arrange for it to be done. All I want is for my parents to live in a nice, safe environment.'

He said, 'Yeah. Right. Leave it with me.'

I left it with him and he did nothing.

The next Christmas I was sitting in the lounge with Ben watching telly, and he was across the road with two of his mates playing around with a car that was up on bricks. He saw me looking at him and he just stared right back and laughed. That was it! I was out of the house and across the road in a flash.

I said to him, 'Me and you need to have a serious talk.'

He said, 'Why bother talking?'

He had a hammer in his hand and he raised it to hit me, so I let him have it! He went down. A split second later, Ben grabbed me from behind. He'd followed me out and was desperate to stop the fight. One of the other guys saw that Ben had got my arms and came at me saying, 'What the fuck are you doing?'

I managed to pull away from Ben before the guy could hit me, and he got one as well. The third fella showed some sense and ran away. Ben grabbed me again and took me back into the house.

I realised that I was in serious trouble. I phoned Dave Robinson and told him what had happened.

'I need you to get round here now,' I said. 'I'm going to be lifted and I need to know that my parents are safe.'

He must have put the phone down and walked straight out of his house, because he arrived before the police did.

I didn't want them in my Mum's house so, when they rang the doorbell, I opened the door, pointed towards the ambulance, said, 'Yep. I did that,' and offered them my wrists. They handcuffed me and took me away.

Unbeknown to me, Dave R. visited all the neighbours to see if anyone had witnessed the event. He wanted to know if anyone had seen the guys attack me and could stand as witnesses on my behalf. Unfortunately, no one had seen anything. I went to court and, thanks to some help from my exceptionally good brief, the judge acknowledged that it was a clear case of self-defence and I walked free.

The prick who didn't care about his neighbours and who had mistaken my politeness for weakness spent several weeks in hospital. The doctors and nurses must have done a good job, because he came out a much-improved neighbour. From then on he kept the noise down and his guttering was faultless!

Chapter 41

CONFLICT

*C*onflict, when it's all boiled down, is very simple. The rule is don't get hit and hit the other person very hard with whatever is available.

I know and practise hundreds of techniques, but in a conflict situation I've only ever used a few simple things. Also, most conflict is about multiples. Most people don't want to fight if they're alone. They want their mates behind them. Often, conflict situations are just about posturing. When they're not, I go back to basics. I just cover and crack 'em, or else I just crack 'em!

Chapter 42

'YOU ARE WANTED ON THE PHONE, SIR'

I was doing quite a lot of door work at this time, but, to tell you the truth, I was useless on the door. People were never going to take any notice of me because I was too small. People who knew me would take notice, but not people who didn't. If I'd been standing on a door telling people what to do, I'd have been fighting all night. So I employed lumps.

However, just because they looked the part, it didn't mean they could fight. To be fair, they could give you a dig if you stood still long enough, but they weren't clever. That said, they didn't need to be, because they looked like a nightmare! I put them at the front, on the door and in the bar, and I'd sit at the back, in a cloakroom, having a coffee. When there was trouble someone would press a buzzer and I'd fly out and sort it.

I used to work a V formation, and I trained my guys how to use it. As soon as it kicked off, I'd go in with two lumps on either side, slightly behind me on an angle, making me the point of the 'V'. So when I went into a crowd, like in a nightclub, they'd come in and split the crowd bigger. I hit the targets in front of me and either threw them behind me or just moved on to the next. Their job was to deal with everyone that I left behind me and to make sure that no one got near my back.

I'd tell them, 'If I get even touched in my back, you'd better make sure I've got no pulse at the end of the day 'cos if I turn round and find out that one of you has let me down you're in big trouble!'

The deal was, I'd manage anything that was in front of me and they would cover everything that was behind me. If I passed the 'item' behind me they had to deal with that, too, and I'd keep going forwards until it was all over. When the V formation works well nobody gets hurt – well, nobody who's working with me, anyway.

I was called to the Playboy club once to eject someone who was being a bit arsy. All the security boys at the Playboy club were ex-police and they wouldn't touch anybody, so if they had a real problem they had to get help in. When I arrived, they pointed out who the guy was and then stood back to let me get on with it. Now, this was the Playboy club so I couldn't go steaming in as I would if there was real trouble kicking off at a normal club. Instead, I went to the guys standing on the door and told them that a man was coming out in a minute and just to let it happen. Then I went down to the foyer and took the phone off the hook. With that done, I walked back upstairs, approached the man and said, 'Excuse me sir, you are wanted on the phone.'

The man looked at me as if I was a piece of shit. 'I beg your pardon?'

'You are wanted on the phone, sir.'

I turned round and walked away. I didn't give him chance to argue and, sure enough, he followed me all the way to the foyer. I picked up the phone and said, 'This is for you, sir.' Then smack! – I hit him straight in the face with it. He went out like a light. I had a friend outside waiting with a car. We picked the guy up, carried him out and threw him in the boot. I just looked at the guys on the door and said, 'You can carry on, now.' Then we drove away.

And the guy in the boot? Let's just say he suffered from – what do they call it in America? – a trunk call!

Minding pubs and clubs was not something that I ever really enjoyed. I did it because I got paid quite well, or friends asked me to help out, and it didn't interfere with my training schedule. What was much more enjoyable was the work I did minding a number of Page Three girls during their outdoor photo shoots. I was employed by an agency. All I had to do was get up at silly o'clock in the morning and stand nearby when the girls took their tops off. My job was to make sure that nobody walked up and touched them. To be fair, though, I often felt like it myself. One of the most lovely girls I've ever seen was Sian Adey-Jones. All the girls were beautiful and photogenic, but Sian was even prettier in real life than she looked in her photos.

The girl with possibly the best personality was Linda Lusardi. I met her at an event to celebrate the opening of a new Mazda dealership in Essex. My karate team and I did a demo and Linda officially opened the place and posed for photos. We got £80 between us and she got a brand-new sports car! Still, I'd never had my picture in the papers – not with my top off, anyway!

Chapter 43

EPPING FOREST

As I look back on it, it's amazing how many of the scrapes I got into were the result of my helping out friends or family. Not that I'm complaining. If the people you are closest to can't rely on you to take their side when there's a problem, what are you worth? Sure, there have been times when some people have been in a bit of trouble and have put my name forward when, perhaps, they didn't need to. And, for a period of time, whenever my phone rang I found myself wondering if it was going to be another person asking for some assistance. However, as I said, people have to know that they can rely on you – no matter what. I have made more than my fair share of mistakes in my life, but the people I care about know that I'm always there for them and that I'll do whatever it takes when they need my help.

One situation that I got into could have turned out very badly for everyone involved. I was asked by a very good friend to give him a hand dealing with a really nasty piece of work. I'm not talking here about a scrapper. No, this guy was a sneak, a liar, a con man and a bully – all the things I particularly dislike in a person. He'd managed to con my friend out of a lot of money, and had done a few other things that were especially distasteful, so I was quite prepared to go with my friend to see if we could talk some sense into this prick. What made it tricky was that the guy was quite elusive, as people of his ilk need to be. It was only after a good deal of searching that we finally caught up with him. We actually ran into him in a stairwell in a block of flats, which wasn't the ideal place for the conversation we needed to have. Fortunately, he realised that now he had no choice but to talk to us and he agreed to go for a drive.

We set off, with my friend sitting in the back seat explaining to the prick that he'd been right out of order. Not surprisingly, the guy came up with every excuse imaginable. My friend was having none of it and started administering some comeuppance. I asked him to cool it. After all, we were driving through a built-up area, with plenty of people around who could look in and see what was going on, and it was my car we were in. I wanted to keep it as clean as possible!

My friend took my advice and suggested we drive out of town. 'Head for the Wake Arms,' he said.

This was a pub I knew well. It was in Epping Forest, about a half-hour drive from where we were. On the way I was obliged to listen to all the shit this guy was accused of doing. There was some really horrible stuff, done to the most defenceless of people, and, as I came to realise just how poisonous he was, I started to get the hump. The prick had been stupid thinking that he could con my friend and get away with it, but some of the individuals whose trust he'd abused had no way of getting him back. I decided that I could do so on their behalf.

By the time we'd reached Epping Forest, I was sure that this guy needed something more than a simple threat. He was too used to hearing, and ignoring, threats. No, what this guy needed was a very convincing lesson. One that he'd never, ever forget!

Before we reached the pub, I pulled off into the forest. At that time, I was working on building sites and I always had a shovel in the boot of my car. I got it out and told the guy to start digging. He became very scared and refused to do as I'd said. My friend threatened to clump him, but still he refused to dig. In the end, we made him strip naked and took all his clothes from him.

I said, 'Go on! Fuck off! And remember, if you do anything to make me bring you back here again, you won't be going home!'

Apparently, after we'd driven off, the guy ran into the middle of the road, stopped a lorry and persuaded the driver to take him to the nearest police station. He rushed inside, wrapped in a blanket that the lorry driver had given him, confessed to a couple of crimes and asked to be arrested there and then! Clearly, he thought he'd be safer in prison than out on the streets. The police, though, knew of this scumbag and guessed what his motives were. Wonderfully, they didn't feel like helping him out.

He was told, 'Sorry, but we don't believe you committed those crimes.'

Basically, the message was, 'We know the score. If some people are wanting to sort you out, that's your problem!'

That was not what the scumbag had expected, and I'm sure it made our promise seem even more powerful. My friend's debts were paid within a couple of days, and then the prick packed his belongings and moved away to infect another part of the country. I doubt that he changed his ways, so I hope that, wherever he went, he met someone else with the antidote for his poison!

Chapter 44

THE HILLS ARE ALIVE WITH THE SOUND OF... GIGGLING

Mike O'Brien, the Chief Instructor of the Karate Union of Wales, was – and still is – a great supporter of my work, and a great friend. He first invited me to Wales in the early 1980s to run a course for his association. He and his lovely wife Mary made me welcome from the very beginning, and I've had the pleasure of their hospitality many times since.

Mike was one of the first Welshmen to practise karate. Although only my height, he had a bodybuilder's physique and had been capped for Wales at rugby. In other words, he was a proper athlete and as hard as nails.

He lived in a beautiful, big property on the side of what he called a mountain and what I insisted was only a hill. My teasing really used to get to him. In all fairness, though, I did agree with him more than I let on – it was nearly half a mountain!

After a hard training session we'd go to the Three Horseshoes pub, which was about two miles away, in the valley below his house. One night, we were walking back from the pub, having drunk lots of Guinness and more than our fair share of brandy, when it was decided that we should have a race. The idea was that we'd sprint between two lampposts, walk between the next two to get our breath back, then sprint again. Now, I am a good sprinter – when I was a schoolkid I represented Essex – but I hate running. That's why I took up karate. Anyway, I agreed and surprised Mike by winning the first race. I surprised him even more by winning the second race, which meant that, as we'd agreed it was going to the best of three, I'd won our little competition. I couldn't stop myself from giggling as we walked between the lampposts before the final sprint. Mike knew that I was fast across a *dojo* floor, but he hadn't expected me to be so quick going up a hill.

I thought to myself, Maybe that's why I'm beating him? He's expecting it to be difficult because he thinks we're running up a mountain. Whereas I know it's only a hill.

I couldn't stop giggling until the final race began – and then I was off like a flash! I sped into the lead, spurred on by the thought of a three–nil victory. It was going to be mine, too, and then disaster struck. As I pulled away from Mike, I had a blowout in my trainer!

(Actually, it was suggested to me later that I just went over on my ankle, but I think my interpretation is more accurate.)

If you've ever seen a car spin out of control when a tyre's burst, you'll find it easy to imagine what happened to me! I went spinning across the road like a madman, totally out of control, and smashed into a low brick wall. The impact broke three of my ribs, but at the time I didn't realise that. I just knew that it hurt like hell. I lay over the top of the wall for several seconds, struggling to get my breath, before Mike's big hands grabbed me and pulled me back onto the road.

We walked the rest of the way home and got a real bollocking from Mary for being late for dinner. As I said earlier, Mike is one of the toughest men you'd ever meet, but he turned into a timid little schoolboy whenever Mary told him off.

The next morning I woke up in real pain. Mike insisted, though, that we go for an early-morning walk. He took me back to the place where I'd crashed into the wall.

'Have a look over there,' he said. 'And imagine what would have happened if you'd flipped over the top when you hit it, or even just decided to roll over onto the grass and rest on the other side.'

I looked. For the second time in less than twenty-four hours the wall took my breath away. There was no grass on the other side. Actually there wasn't much of anything, just a two-hundred-foot drop! If I'd gone over the wall I'd definitely have been resting for a very long time – which just shows you how dangerous a blowout in your trainer can be!

Another time Mike and I staggered back from the Three Horseshoes, had dinner and a few more drinks, and then he decided, crazily, that we ought to go out and do something adventurous.

Mike was well into the outdoors thing. He used to run a lot of outdoor-pursuits activities with different groups of people. He was also big mates with Lofty Wiseman, a

teacher Sensei Keinosuke Enoeda.

Two of my heroes – Senseis Andy Sherry and Terry O'Neill and me as a young pup. The first England Kata Team at the European Championships.

bove: The Great Britain team at the World Championships. I am the third from the *ht back row, just behind Sensei.

low: Ready for action at the Championships. I'm at the front.

Above: The JKA Instructors class 1977. Don't look for me, I'm taking the photo.

Below: The young guns (left to right) Tase Matasan, Ronnie Ross, me and Ray Kerridg

bove: The Brighton Dojo – great days!

low: In 1990 I returned to Japan to train on a *gasshuku* – a summer training camp –
n by Yahara Sensei.

Above: Enoeda Sensei in action.

Below: A very proud day for me. I present Enoeda Sensei's wife, Reiko, with a photo o
her husband she had never seen before. Sensei looks over us from the photo behind.

ove: Chris Parker, co-author of this book. A good friend and an exceptional artial artist.

low: My good friend and former World Champion Aidan Trimble receiving his 7th dan.

Above: Me and Simon getting up close and personal.

Below: Me at work.

former member of the SAS, whose books about survival have been a big success. Lofty led teams into the Brecon Beacons, testing their physical and mental stamina, teaching them how to survive when the going got tough.

This particular night, Mike 'Mr Macho' O'Brien decided, at about 1 a.m., after a Chinese meal, Guinness, vodka and brandy, that life would be much more fun if we spent the remaining hours of darkness under the stars somewhere on the hill – sorry, mountain.

Who was I to argue? So, along with Buck, Mike's massive German Shepherd dog, we left the warmth of the house and set off through the night with only two sleeping bags and my bottle of vodka for comfort.

After trekking uphill for quite some time we came across several large nets fastened about eight feet above the ground between several trees. It was a place where people on outward-bound courses worked higher up in the trees, and the nets were there to catch them if they fell. They were, quite literally, safety nets – although they didn't prove to be that safe for us.

Mike told me to watch closely as he demonstrated how to get into the nets. He reached up and took hold of the netting with an underhand grip, as if he were going to do a chin-up, then pulled himself up and did a forward roll into the net. However, Mike was keen to show off, and we had been drinking all night, and it was pitch black, so, instead of rolling to the middle of the net, he kept going – right across the netting and straight off the other side!

All I heard was, 'Aaargh!' followed by a thump as he hit the ground. A few seconds later he came staggering towards me with his face cut and twigs in his hair.

'I think I was showing off a bit too much,' he said.

'Fucking right,' I agreed.

The second time, Mike rolled into the net and stayed there. I was right behind him. Buck curled up on the ground. He clearly found it easier to settle down than we did. Two men lying in a large net might start out well away from each other, but it isn't long before they both slide into the middle. That's what happened to us. Before I knew it we were almost shoulder to shoulder.

'I'm not kissing you goodnight,' I said.

'Too true,' he replied.

We did share the vodka, though, as we lay there, looking up at the stars, telling funny stories, giggling like naughty schoolboys. Suddenly, I heard a rustling noise below us. Buck jumped to his feet.

'What the fuck is that?' I whispered.

Mary's voice cut through the darkness. 'Mike O'Brien?'

'Yes, Mary.'

'What do you think you're doing? You're like two ten-year-old children! Now get yourselves down here and get to bed!'

'Yes, Mary. Sorry, Mary.'

By the time we'd climbed out of the net, Mary was already on her way back to the house. Buck was at her heel, with his head bowed, thinking that he was in trouble, too. We followed them home – and went straight to bed without saying another word. Sometimes you just have to know when to do as you're told.

Chapter 45

BLACK FERRARI

For a period of time I had a relationship with the ex-wife of a member of a well-known band. She studied karate and we met during a course at Crystal Palace. She was black, beautiful and a talented singer in her own right. Her stage name was Mercedes. As I'm sure you are aware by now, I've always appreciated both women and cars. So guess how lucky I felt meeting Mercedes.

Actually, I felt luckier than you might imagine, because she also had a black and beautiful Ferrari. And, when she went over to America to do some recording, she asked me if I'd like to look after it. I agreed as reluctantly as I possibly could – which, to be honest, was not very.

In one sense, though, it was a mistake. The car was fabulous, but it cost me more than I could have bargained for. All my weekly wages went on petrol. Plus at least one instructor who'd booked me for a course, saw me turn up in a Ferrari, decided that I was doing too bloody well, thank you very much, and never booked me again!

I should have had a sticker in the car that read, 'It's only on loan.'

In hindsight, I could have put that sticker on a lot of things in my life. For example, it seems that not even the most important relationships last for ever. Even when they stop and start again...

Chapter 46

'I HEARD THAT'

It came as a real surprise to me when, right out of the blue, Enoeda Sensei's secretary phoned to say that he wanted to meet me. My answer was immediate.

'Yes! When and where?'

She told me and, as I always do when I'm meeting someone, I arrived early. Enoeda Sensei walked in dead on time. I bought him a drink and we sat down. He asked how I was.

'Fine, Sensei.'

'You still training?'

'Yeah.'

He nodded. 'I heard that. Do you have your own club?'

'No, Sensei.'

He nodded again. 'Yes, I heard that. Have you joined another association?'

'No, Sensei.'

'I heard that, too.' He paused. 'We had a small problem in the past.'

'Yes, we did.'

'Anyway,' he said. 'I think we forget about that now and move on.' He slapped me on my knee. 'What do you say?'

'I think that's a very good idea, Sensei.'

'Good! I think you should come and train in my *dojo*, and help me out. What do you think?'

'I'd be very happy to, Sensei.'

'Good! When will you come?'

'Tomorrow!'

'Good!'

And the next night there I was. You could have heard a pin drop when I walked into the *dojo*. The good guys, like Craig Raye, came up and greeted me straightaway. Most people, though, didn't know what to do. They didn't know about our meeting and wondered how Enoeda Sensei would react when he walked in and saw me. When he did enter, I made sure that I bowed before everyone else.

He beamed and returned my greeting. Then everyone knew it was all right. I was back in the fold!

PART 4

SENSEI
(*Sensei*: a teacher, literally 'one who has gone before')
1986-2003

Chapter 47

AN AMERICAN TAKEAWAY

I used to spend a lot of time in Portsmouth teaching for, and training with, Mick Dewey. After training we'd always go to a restaurant called the Chinese Centre. Mick was well known there. The boss loved him and we were treated very well. On this particular occasion, Mick's brother-in-law, Mervyn, who was one of the seniors in Mick's karate association, was with us. Portsmouth is a naval base and, at this time, the American fleet were in.

We were sitting in our normal seats by the window, minding our own business and having a nice time when two American sailors started complaining about their meal. The Chinese waiters were used to scraps in the restaurant and they knew what they were doing. If you had too much of a row with them they would come out of the kitchen waving their little hatchets. It was always funny to watch. The Americans became more and more belligerent. They started throwing rice and other bits and pieces around, shouting out, 'I'm not fucking paying for this!'

Mick and I were watching, waiting for the kitchen doors to open and the hatchets to come out. Mervyn was going, 'Come on, let's just have our meal,' when the Americans suddenly got up and kicked the chairs and tables all over the place. It didn't affect us, so we just sat there. They kicked a door open, which smashed, and went outside. They must have thought they'd got away with it, but the next minute all the Chinese came flying out the kitchen – whoosh! – waving their little bits and pieces. Now Mick and I were half smiling and half on edge.

All of a sudden the window came in. Boom! There were bits of glass everywhere. Now it was affecting us!

I said to Mick, 'That's it! I've fucking well had enough of this. I'm going outside.'

As I got off the seat, Mick was with me. Mervyn didn't move. He was always very calm.

We got outside to find a semicircle of Chinese around one of the Americans. He was a lump, about six foot two or three tall and a fit looking-boy. The other one was smaller, and he'd got only two or three Chinese around him.

I went straight through the semicircle and – whack! – I punched the fit-looking guy so hard he went out like a light. I actually hit him that hard that he fell forwards onto me. By then my blood was up. Mick had got hold of the other little dickhead and was rattling him against the wall. I pushed the other Chinese out of the way, got in front of Mick, and butted the guy. Bang!

All I heard from Mick was, 'You greedy bastard!'

The Chinese got hold of the big American – there were two on each leg – and dragged him back into the restaurant. Served him right, I thought, because now he was getting cut on all the glass that he'd smashed. A nice bit of comeuppance!

Mick picked up the other fella and escorted him in by the scruff of his neck and the seat of his pants. We threw them both down at the end of the restaurant.

The boss had already phoned the American Military Police. He'd had so much trouble in there that he knew the number.

Mick and I walked back to our table and sat down. Merv said, 'You haven't left the table as far as I'm concerned.'

I said, 'All right, Merv.'

He went on, 'And I've kept your dinners warm.'

Which was true, but not in a way that was of any good to us. He'd eaten half of the dinners, that's what he'd done, and now they were warm inside his stomach!

All of a sudden, the door opened and two American military policemen walked in. You know those cartoons of a big bulldog, with a great big neck and a chain, held by a fella with a big, square jaw, a tiny waist and an upper body that goes out in such a large V that his shoulders are miles out of proportion? Well these two American policemen were just like that. But one was bigger than the other!

I said to Mick, 'Fucking hell, Mick! Have a look at what's just come in.'

They looked the part all right, all tooled up with batons and protective gear, and you could tell by their manner and the way they moved that they were the part.

The bigger one said, 'Who's done that to our boys?'

The restaurant boss pointed at us and the smaller of the

two sailors, the one who could speak, said, 'Those fuckers done it!'

The policemen looked at us and drew their truncheons.

I thought, 'Oh, fucking hell!'

At which point the bigger policeman hit the sailor who'd just spoken over the head with his truncheon. Then, with one big hand, he reached down and grabbed the lapels of the guy I'd knocked unconscious. He pushed him up against the wall and proceeded to lift him off his feet and put him over his shoulder. It was incredible! It was like lifting a very heavy dead weight using one arm and no apparent effort. He handled this big guy as if he were a baby. And all the while he kept watching us. And we kept watching him. Christ, he was a lump! Actually he was a lump with a truncheon, but I had a chopstick and I would have been quicker than him. That said, I was impressed with his demeanour and attitude, with the way he dealt with the sailor and the way he looked at us. At no point did he suggest, 'You're next.' He just did his job and let us know he was good at it.

His mate dragged the other sailor out and, while Mick and me watched them go, Merv continued to make sure our food was warm.

People often ask me if I'm impressed with size. The answer is, 'Yes. I'm often impressed with size, but when push comes to shove – fuck it!'

What impressed me more than the MP's large muscles was the fact that I went into a Chinese restaurant and watched an American takeaway! How many people can say they've done that?

Chapter 48

THE BRIGHTON DOJO

Mick Dewey phoned me to say that he was considering leaving the KUGB and creating a new organisation with his brother-in-law, Mervyn. Things had come to a head in the southern region and Mick wanted to know if I would still teach for him if he set up on his own. I told him that it was guaranteed. Then he asked, 'If it grows, will you become involved?'

I said, 'Yeah, of course.'

As time went on Mick's organisation, which he called SEKU – Shotokan of England Karate Union – did grow. This was no surprise to me, it's what you'd expect with someone like Mick in charge. So, in 1985, he asked me to join him. There were things that Mick wanted me to do within the association and there were things that I wanted to do, too. For example, I wanted to establish a special instructors' class, to be held once a month, based on what I'd experienced in Japan. Mick thought that was a great idea and, when we'd agreed some other things, I accepted his invitation to join SEKU as the Technical Director.

I was living in London at the time and I said to Mick, 'Put a needle in a map somewhere down south and I'll go and live there and open a *dojo*.'

He replied, 'I can do better than that. You've been teaching regularly at the Brighton *dojo* for a while now. Why not take that over?'

The Brighton *dojo* was run by a group of seniors, Will Davis, Greg Weedakin, Paul Bonnet and John Cave, who took turns teaching. They were all great *karateka*, but none of them wanted to be the main teacher. Instead, they just wanted to concentrate on their own training. I met them in a small hotel to discuss the proposition of my taking over.

I said, 'You need to understand that, if the *dojo* is mine, it's mine. If you get me in to run the club you're going to have to hand it over to me lock, stock and barrel. It will be run professionally.'

Of course, they had some requirements of their own, but within ten minutes the deal was done and we were buying each other a drink.

Paul Bonnet was an estate agent and he found me a place to live in Hove. I moved there in December 1985 and began teaching officially in January 1986. It was the start of a fantastic period in my life.

The *dojo* was a hall in the Cardinal Newman school. It was an adults-only *dojo*. I didn't teach kids, only people over sixteen, and most of the students were senior grades. At its peak I think we had forty *dan* grades and about twenty juniors. Although even our juniors were better than their grades suggested.

While the *dojo* had a good reputation when I took over, within five years it had developed a fantastic reputation. It was to become so well known that karate students from the JKA were told that, when visiting England, they ought to train at Enoeda Sensei's *dojo* at Marshall Street and my Brighton *dojo*. I thought that was really nice.

I was, of course, very choosy about who was let in. Newcomers had to sit and watch for a couple of weeks and then I'd let them know if they could join. Also, I wouldn't let any conflict occur in the club. Remember, by this time I'd had lots of experience of how to run a karate club both with Enoeda Sensei and in Japan. I told everyone, 'If there's a conflict between any of you, no matter what your grade is or who started it, I'll sling you both out.'

I wanted all the students to be loyal. I was going to give them my very best and, in return, I wanted the best from them.

For example, I'd take six weeks to teach one *kata*. I'd spend half an hour in each class teaching one sequence from a *kata*, or how to apply the moves against an opponent. So if someone missed a class they couldn't cope with the next one. That was fine by me. I wasn't prepared to be fucked about. If a student chose to have a session or two off just because he wanted to, I then gave him an additional session or two off just because I wanted to! One guy took a month off training without telling me. When he returned to the *dojo* I gave him another month off. He said, 'But I'm ready to come back now.'

I said, 'Yeah, but I'm not ready to have you!'

As you can gather, I ran a really tight ship at Brighton.

Rules were rules and they had to be followed. One rule, for example, was that the first person in the *dojo* had to begin cleaning the floor. The next person in, if they were junior in rank – which they were going to be because I was nearly always the first one to arrive – had to take over. There are three things you need to understand here. First, the *dojo* floor is like our church, so we treat it with respect. Second, it was a school hall and we were running around on it with bare feet, so there were obvious hygiene issues. Third, I wanted my students to recognise, and act upon, the responsibilities that come with holding each grade.

I always told them, 'With rank comes kudos. With kudos comes responsibility. Seniors, therefore, have a responsibility to look after juniors.'

My view was that every yellow belt in the club had a responsibility to make sure that, for example, every red belt (the grade below yellow) tied his belt correctly. If he didn't, the red belt would get a telling-off and the yellow belt would get fifty press-ups. I made sure that each grade was responsible for the grade below it.

The first time students forgot to clean the floor I'd been in Brighton for only a couple of weeks and I was determined to make a point. At the start of a karate class people kneel down and bow, and I knew that on this occasion it would make the knees of my crisp, white *gi* dirty. Still, I figured I could use that. After the bow, I stood up and looked pointedly at the dirt on my trousers. Everyone realised that I wasn't happy.

I didn't bother with the usual warm-up. Instead I told them to face a partner. I could see them thinking, Oh shit! because they expected to start fighting.

They were wrong, though. I made one partner lie down on his back and the other one drag him across the *dojo* by his ankles. Then they reversed it. Everyone did this three times. By then the floor was clean and the backs of their *gis* were filthy.

I told them, 'When you get home, see how difficult that is to wash out!'

I can remember only one other time when students forgot to clean the *dojo* floor. I walked in and felt a slight layer of dust beneath my feet. 'Has the floor been done?' I asked, knowing that it hadn't. The junior grades legged it immediately to the cupboard to get the broom.

The problem they'd got was that I always started a class precisely on time, which meant that the floor couldn't be cleaned before I was ready to begin.

'Enough!' I said to a young white belt who was clutching the broom. 'Get it away!' He ran over to the cupboard while everyone else lined up.

After about five minutes I realised that the white belt wasn't in the class. I thought to myself, Where can he be? And then something made me check inside the cupboard. Sure enough, there he was!

I said to him, 'What are you doing in here?'

He replied, 'When I heard you say, "Line up" I knew that I couldn't get back into the line in time, so I thought I'd better stay here.'

I was amazed! 'Were you planning to stay here throughout the class?' I asked.

He shrugged. 'I was wondering when the best time might be to come out,' he said.

'It's now,' I told him. And a very red-faced white belt joined the others.

It was at the Brighton *dojo* that, I believe, I learned how to teach. The great thing was, because it was my own *dojo*, I taught what I wanted to in the way I wanted to. I was able to put more thought into a long-term strategy, rather than the more short-term approach you have to take when you do a weekend course for someone else. Then you have to respect what the host wants. It's a bit like doing a stage show. You have to perform some of the old favourites, giving people at least some of what they expect, and there's no real chance to develop anything new. At Brighton, though, I had the time to develop what I was doing. I learned how to convey all the knowledge I'd got. I had time to analyse how I was operating and find ways to improve it.

I know there were a lot of people who thought I was a decent instructor anyway, but I never felt comfortable being called an instructor until about 1988. By then I was just about ready to accept it when people called me 'Sensei'. Before then I'd thought that the title 'Sensei' belonged only to people like Enoeda Sensei and Andy Sherry, individuals like that who were my seniors. Nowadays, in some quarters, things have changed completely. There are many people now who are willing to adorn others with titles – and just as many who are willing to accept them! As a result, there are so many people in the martial-arts world with grand titles like *Shihan* and 'Master' associated with their name. The only person I've ever referred to as 'Master' is Nakayama Sensei. He had truly achieved that status. Even Enoeda Sensei refused to let any of his students refer to him as 'Master'. Today there's just too much ego involved.

Chapter 49

TEACHING

*T*here are certain ways of looking at teaching. If it's a course, I may ask the guy who's hired me, 'Is there anything you want me to cover?' And they often give me some direction. You can never go to a course with an iron-clad idea of what you're going to do, because you might find that the students either can't cope with it or are better than that. So you have to design the content around the capabilities of the students – just stretch them enough within their boundaries.

Wherever I'm teaching, whether it's with my own students or those from a different organisation, I'm always guided by what Enoeda Sensei taught me. He said, 'Start with a bang! Any teaching you do, do in the middle of the session. Then end with a bang!'

And that's what I do. I look to make my classes interesting, exciting and inspiring. I've been called an 'entertainer' by quite a few people because I might joke and smile during a class. I don't wear a fierce face when I teach, unless someone gives me a reason to. If students are terrified of the instructor and, therefore, of making mistakes, they don't learn well. If you think about it, the instructor has to manage the emotional state of the students.

So, I work out very quickly what level the students are at and then I put together a combination of techniques that I know most of them can't quite do yet, but they can learn. I get the class buzzing, make sure their enthusiasm and energy levels are high, and then break the combination down into little sections – like bits of a puzzle – and teach one section at a time. At the end of the class I put the entire sequence back together and the students go through it with a partner and then on their own. I tell them how well they are doing. I make sure they realise what improvements they've made. I send them out feeling great, believing in themselves and wanting more. It's simple, really.

Chapter 50

'SENSEI, ALL I WANT IS YOUR FEET ON MY DOJO FLOOR'

The only *dojo* that Enoeda Sensei would teach at in England that was outside the KUGB was my Brighton *dojo*. I remember getting up the courage to ask him if he'd visit and when I did he just smiled and said, 'Oh, yes!'

He came down several times and never once charged me a fee – which cost me an absolute fortune! You see, there was no way that my Boss was coming down to my *dojo* unless his visit was perfect in every way. Anyone who knows me will know that I'm something of a perfectionist anyway and every one of Enoeda Sensei's visits turned into a major event. I checked every possible avenue to make sure that it all worked out according to plan. I checked the route to and from the train station – I didn't want Sensei to drive, so I always sent him a first-class rail ticket. I booked him into a suite at the Grand Hotel and checked the room before his arrival. I got the room keys early so that he didn't have to bother with reception. I gave the concierge a drink to make sure that he was straight out to the car when we arrived. I had my car cleaned immaculately. I arranged for a local fishmonger to buy Sensei's favourite fish. I booked the best table in the best Chinese restaurant in town and told the chef precisely how to cook Sensei's meal. Mick always came down the day before and stopped over to help me make sure that everything was right.

The class itself was for black belts and by invitation only. I had students arrive at the *dojo* an hour before the lesson was due to start to clean the floor. Before the class Sensei said to me, 'Dabie, what do you want me to teach?'

I answered simply, 'Whatever you like, Sensei. All I want is your feet on my *dojo* floor.'

I got that and so much more. When Enoeda Sensei walked in to teach his first class in my Brighton *dojo* there were sixty of the best black belts in the south of England desperate for his instruction. And I was one of them.

A couple of days later Paul Bonnet was telling me how much he had enjoyed Sensei's class and how shocked Will Davis had been by my attitude during it.

I asked him why.

He said, 'When Will partnered you for sparring, you scared him to death. He told me that there wasn't a crack in your face. That you were completely different to how you are when you are teaching us.'

Of course I was! They were used to me being in charge, thinking only about them and their development. But when Enoeda Sensei was teaching I was there as his student – and nobody was going to do better in his class than me!

231

On another occasion Enoeda Sensei phoned me two days before he was due to come down, to inform me that he'd badly torn his calf muscle. 'I'm sorry, Dabie,' he said. 'I will have to cancel.'

This was really bad news. Not only was I really looking forward to seeing him, but also all the arrangements had been made. I said, 'Sensei, I don't care. Just come and stand there. You don't have to do anything.'

He paused briefly, then said, 'OK. I'll come, but you must teach.'

I agreed, put the phone down and then thought about what he'd just asked. Suddenly it was like being a kid again. All the nerves kicked in. I felt the way I used to before I went training with him.

I told Mick what was happening and asked if he'd mind not training – after all, Mick is my senior. He agreed to sit with Sensei during the class, and I did my best to prepare myself.

On the day itself I drove Sensei to the class, as usual. He noticed that I was nervous – probably because of the way I was gripping the steering wheel.

'What is the matter?' he asked.

'I'm a little bit scared, Sensei,' I confessed. 'I've never taught a class in front of you before.'

He nodded. 'Pull over,' he said.

I did.

Then he said, 'Me, too. I'm also a little bit nervous. I've never seen one of my students teach before.'

It had never occurred to me until that moment, but, if you think about it, every time he was in the *dojo* he taught the class. We had a quiet word together, he assured me that we would both be OK and we set off for the *dojo*.

My nervousness stayed with me until I tied my belt. Then, as always happens, everything else was forgotten and I prepared to go to work. It's an interesting thing, but it doesn't matter how I'm feeling or what's in my mind – I can be injured or ill or have some problem that needs resolving – but, as soon as I tie the knot on my belt, the only thing in mind is karate. Aches, sprains and concerns all disappear and I'm ready for anything.

We'd put out a table for Sensei and Mick to sit at and, as I was warming the class up, I was aware of them whispering to each other. They stopped once I'd got the class buzzing and they didn't speak again until we'd finished.

Sensei didn't comment on the class until that night, when we went to the restaurant for dinner. He said, 'Dabie, I'm very, very proud. Very good condition and very good teaching. You can do everything.'

Well, I needed scaffolding for my head. What a compliment!

Chapter 51

TAKING THE PISS

I don't always teach alone. I've worked with a number of excellent instructors over the years. One man I've worked very closely with, whom I'm privileged to call my very good friend, is Aidan Trimble, the charismatic and dynamic former world Shotokan karate champion.

I'd always wanted to meet Aidan and was finally introduced to him by Simon Oliver, a Nottingham-based *karateka* for whom I've run many courses. We met in a nightclub and spent the rest of the evening talking about karate. We hit it off together straightaway. Everything I'd heard about him was true. We became so involved in our conversation that we didn't realise when it was throwing-out time. According to Simon, the bouncers didn't want to come near us. They knew who Aidan was, and they had spent the night watching us demonstrating moves to each other. Anyway, we finally got the hint and left.

It was the start of an important relationship in my life. If it wasn't for Aidan, I wouldn't have written a karate book or made a series of instructional DVDs. We also work very well together. When I was offered the chance to teach with him in Cork, Ireland, I took it instantly.

The first day's training went really well. About ten minutes before the end, one of the senior Irish instructors put his hand up and asked if he could be excused for a couple of minutes. I guessed he needed a piss and let him go. Two minutes later he was back. I frowned and looked at Aidan, because people usually know better than to go in and out of my classes. Aidan just smiled. He'd taught there before, so I thought, OK, he knows the way it works here. I'll talk to him afterwards.

I realised later that the guy hadn't needed to piss – he'd gone to the bar to order the first six pints of Murphy's, because it took so long to pour them correctly. Demonstrating typical Irish hospitality, he'd wanted to make sure that mine and Aidan's drinks were ready the instant we finished teaching.

The venue was a small community hall, without any changing rooms. So, when we entered the bar we were still wearing our *gis*. The same guy was waiting for us. 'Your pint is ready for you, sir,' he said, putting it on the table in front of me.

I said to Aidan, 'Let's not go mad here. Just a quick pint and then back to the hotel to get washed and changed for dinner.'

Four hours later we were still there. But now I'd got Murphy's down the front of my *gi* and every pint came with a Jameson's whiskey. I was pickled. With my bladder bursting, I got up eventually and wandered into the loo for a piss. Anyone who has ever worn a karate *gi* knows that there's no fly in the trousers, which means they're not the easiest thing to control while you're standing up weeing. What makes it even more awkward is that you've got a large, thick belt to undo and hold somewhere. When you've had a skinful of Irish stout and whiskey, the whole process is even more challenging.

So, there I was, having a pee. I'd undone my *gi* bottoms and had flexed my legs outwards to keep the trousers gripped halfway down my thighs. I'd loosened my belt and had one end between my teeth to make sure it didn't fall to the floor. My best friend was in my hand and I was enjoying the pleasure that comes only with the moment of much-needed release, when I caught a blur of movement out of the corner of my eye.

There was a fist coming at my head!

It made me forget instantly about the need to keep my trousers up or my belt in my mouth. It even made me forgot about the need to control the constant stream of processed Murphy's that was pouring out of me. I simply parried the punch, saw a face and elbowed it. The guy screamed and collapsed. I looked down and saw that it was one of the black belts from the class! I pulled him to his feet and said, 'What the fuck are you doing?'

He said, 'I just wanted to see if you could do it outside the *dojo*, Sensei.'

I said, 'Now you know that I can.' And I slapped him again.

Back in the bar, I said to Aidan, 'You'll never guess what this guy's just done.'

Aidan grinned and said, 'He's tried to have a pop at you.'

I was amazed. 'How the hell do you know that?'

Aidan's grin widened, 'Because he tried it on me last year. I was stood at the bar and he had a go. I had to back-kick him.'

'Why the fuck didn't you warn me?'

Aidan roared with laughter and I realised that, if I'd been here with Mick Dewey, I wouldn't have told him either. If anyone had been taking the piss, it wasn't Aidan. It was the black belt who thought I couldn't fight unless my *gi* was fastened.

Chapter 52

HAPPY BIRTHDAY TO ME!

I really loved my flat in Hove. It was a smashing little place, on a quiet, one-way, crescent really close to the seafront. On this particular occasion, which was just before Christmas, I'd pulled out in my car – a beautiful Audi 80 – with only a casual glance behind me, which was why I didn't see the delivery man on a motorbike who was far too close for comfort. He swerved, I braked, between us we managed to miss each other. Understandably, he wasn't too happy. He jumped off his bike and I got out of my Audi. I held my hands up and apologised. He called me a wanker. I told him that the near-miss had been my fault, and that whether I was a wanker or not was irrelevant. He swore at me, booted the front wing of my car, and drove off. I do my best to be honest at all times. It isn't always easy, because sometimes people don't want to hear what you've got to say and sometimes today's honesty is tomorrow's regret. This prick, though, took my honesty as weakness – and that really is a mistake.

I was back in my Audi in a flash! I didn't bother following him round the crescent. The best way to be sure of catching him was to drive to the other end of the crescent and then go the wrong way round the one-way street. That was what I did and I found him, parked, getting ready to make a delivery.

This cheeky bastard thought that he could wilfully damage someone's car and carry on as if nothing had happened. I jumped out of the Audi with a very specific intention in mind. I wanted to get his name, address and insurance details, your honour...

He was a tall, slim guy wearing black leathers and a crash helmet. I said to him, 'OK, arsehole. You've been pretty good at kicking my car. Do you fancy a shot at me?'

He did.

He walked straight towards me, taking his helmet off as he came.

I said, 'Do yourself a favour and leave it on.' I wasn't being daft in saying that. It allowed me to do what I wanted without causing him too much damage and, more importantly, I knew that it obscured his vision. I couldn't believe it, though, when he took my advice.

As he got closer he raised his hands. I thought, Here comes Christmas!

I covered both his arms and hit him with *teisho* – palm heel – on the side of his helmet. (That wasn't a groin shot, by the way, it was his crash helmet that I slammed!) Then I grabbed him by the neck, swept his legs, picked him up and threw him over a three foot high wall.

He screamed and disappeared.

I thought, Fuck me! What's happened here?

I looked over the wall and saw that it had a six-foot drop on the other side. I realised at that point that I wasn't going to get his insurance details. I decided to leave him resting and call it evens.

I did wonder whether there was going to be a comeback, but when nothing happened after a couple of weeks I figured it was all over.

I couldn't have been more wrong.

It all kicked off again on 4 March. I remember the date so clearly because it was my birthday.

I was at home, opening cards and reading messages from family and friends, who were wishing me health and happiness, when the doorbell rang. I thought, I bet it's a parcel, with a message that says 'Happy birthday, Hazard!'

Oh no, it wasn't! I opened the door to see two policemen standing there. One of them said, 'David Frederick Hazard?'

I said, 'Yes.' Thinking to myself, This has to be a hell of a present – the police have had to deliver it.

I was wrong again.

The policeman said, 'You're nicked!'

They took me down to the police station, where they asked for my date of birth. I told them and they all looked at each other, paused for a second, and sang me 'Happy Birthday'. Then they locked me up!

My good friend Aidan Trimble came down to offer a character reference when it went to court. He explained that I'd used only reasonable force and that a man with my skills could have been much more violent if the situation had called for it.

The arsehole was claiming compensation, because he'd had to take time off work. He'd even brought his damaged crash helmet in as evidence. Fortunately for me, I'd been able to employ a Queen's Counsel. He pointed out that I was a thirty-five-year-old man, of less than average height and only medium build, who'd been up against a younger, bigger, threatening, leather-clad biker. The judge agreed that it was clearly a case of self-defence, and the case was thrown out.

Only then did I find out that the delivery man who'd taken a fall was a police special constable!

Chapter 53

DOPEHEADS, SHEEP AND A VAN LOAD OF RIOT POLICE

My flat was on the first floor. The guy who lived in the basement had all sorts of problems. He had lost one leg and, more importantly, received quite severe brain damage as a result of a motorbike accident. Although he'd been awarded lots of money as compensation, he was unable to manage it properly. To make matters worse, he was also a drug addict. At the local rehabilitation centre he met lots of other drug addicts who quickly realised that he wasn't the full ticket. They swarmed all over him. He got mugged, beaten up and stolen from on a regular basis. I'd phoned the police and social services several times, but nothing had been done. Sometimes I'd hear him screaming at two or three o'clock in the morning and rush downstairs only to find that he was just freaking out. You never knew when he was being threatened, beaten up or just having a bad mind trip.

One day, I came back from teaching a class and saw a couple of dopeheads standing outside his door. I asked them what they were doing. They told me to mind my own fucking business. I told them to leave the lad alone and go. One of them got a bit saucy, so I gave him a slap. The other one didn't want to know and they both left.

Not for long, though. They came back the next day with another of their dopehead friends. Someone had obviously come up with the very stupid idea that if there were three of them they'd be able to sort me out, and the other two had, equally stupidly, gone along with it. Oh, well, you know what they say about the best-laid schemes of dopeheads and men?

I was outside cleaning my car – a big, blue Merc – chatting to a neighbour called Terry, when they made their comeback. Terry was a lovely fella. He was in his sixties and not in the best of health, but he was the sort of guy who'd do anything for anyone. He worked as a handyman and part-time actor. When I tell you that he was employed through an agency called The Uglys, you'll realise that he wasn't a Brad Pitt lookalike!

Anyway, I was telling Terry about the two guys I'd sent on their way when he looked over my shoulder and said, 'Hold up, Dave! I think you've got a return visit.'

I turned round and, sure enough, there they were, three of them standing on the corner of the road, watching me. After a bit of hurried conversation one crossed the road and started walking towards me, while the other two approached on the other side.

Terry said, 'This doesn't look good!'

I said, 'No, it don't. They've come for a kick-off. Do yourself a favour and go indoors.'

Terry did as he was told. Unbeknown to me, as soon as he was inside he called the police. He probably thought that I needed protection and, in his mind, was doing the right thing. As it happens, he was making the situation a whole lot worse. It wasn't his fault, though. It was the fault of the sheep at Shoreham. Or, to be more accurate, the fault of the people at Shoreham who were protesting about the way the sheep were being transported. If the protestors hadn't been protesting in a violent manner the riot police wouldn't have been at Shoreham. If the riot police hadn't been at Shoreham, which is only two minutes' drive from where I lived, they wouldn't have been able to send a van load of them in response to Terry's call. And then I wouldn't have had to throw one of them into a wall.

Anyway, I'm getting ahead of myself. With Terry safely out of the way, I turned my attention to the dopeheads. The guy on his own was walking with one arm stiff and one arm swinging normally. So I knew he was carrying. One of the others had his hand inside his jacket. So I knew he was, too. I decided to seize the advantage and I went at them.

I moved more quickly than they did, both mentally and physically, and by the time they realised that I was on them it was too late. The one guy tried to pull a huge carving knife out of his jacket. He must have tired himself out doing it, because he fell asleep a split second later. The knife clattered to the ground. The guy next to him also caught the sleeping bug and collapsed. Actually, the first one had caught a good right hand and the second one caught a spinning elbow. Still, two dopeheads fast asleep together in the middle of the road – how sweet is that?

The third guy must have been right out of his head on something, because he saw what had happened to his mates and still kept coming. As he crossed the road, he slid a chair leg out of his coat sleeve.

I thought, That isn't fair! The poor little sod in the basement flat has only got one leg, and this bastard's got three!

I moved towards him, keen to teach him a lesson. He should have brought a bed to this fight, not a chair leg, because he was definitely going to sleep.

But that was when the riot police arrived. The dopehead saw half a dozen policemen with shields, helmets, batons – the lot – come rushing out of this van and did the most appropriate thing for a man with three legs. He legged it.

Two of the coppers gave chase and I bent down to pick the knife up. That was my first mistake. The police had arrived to see two guys unconscious at my feet, a third running away and me reaching for a blade. They came to absolutely the wrong conclusion and charged at me, waving their batons. One of them decided to be a real hero and came in swinging. I covered his arms, put my foot against his lower leg and sent him spinning into a wall. That was my second mistake. All of a sudden I've got three riot police standing around me, batons raised, shouting, 'Get on your knees! Get on your knees!'

Thankfully, a sergeant arrived at that point and calmed everything down. I was allowed back into my flat, where I told the sergeant what had happened. He listened carefully and looked pointedly at the collection of martial-arts weapons and karate memorabilia that were on show. When he'd got my version of events, he went outside and spoke to the dopeheads. I couldn't believe the result.

'They want to press charges against you,' he said.

'What?'

'I know that you want to press charges against them, too. And if you do you'll almost certainly win, but you'll gain nothing. In fact, you'll lose money. They can't afford to pay your costs and I very much doubt if they'll get locked up.' The sergeant shrugged. 'I'm afraid that's the reality of it. I suggest you just call it quits.'

'Great! And what happens if they come back tomorrow after another dose of heroin even more mob-handed than they were today?'

The sergeant glanced at my samurai swords. 'Looking round your flat, I'd say you could probably deal with it.' He stood up, ready to leave. 'And next time do yourself a favour – don't let anyone call the police!'

Chapter 54

CONTROL THE SPACE

*I*n a conflict situation it's essential that you control the space. You must make the environment yours. You must change it quickly and then act before anyone else has chance to adjust. If you think about what I did with the dopeheads, you'll realise that I controlled and changed the distance by moving towards them faster than they were coming at me. It's always a good ploy, because it changes the other person's perspective, which creates a brief, emotional shock. During that time, even if it lasts only for a second, they are unable to react efficiently. That creates the one chance you need.

Another way to control the space is to move more slowly towards your opponent than they are moving to you. If your opponent is posturing and clearly ready to fight, combine this slower movement with a smile as you close in on them. This usually brings them down and makes them relax. In that instant – clump them!

Chapter 55

FLAT-FACED BASTARD AND SAGGY-ARSE FACE

I first met Karen, one of the great loves of my life, in Inverness in 1986. She was a brown belt, training on a weekend course and, while I was impressed with her effort and commitment, I was far more impressed with how she looked. She was beautiful.

I hadn't had a serious and stable relationship with a woman since Deborah's departure a few years earlier, and I had no intention of starting another one – until I saw Karen. She was training hard, she looked amazing, and I couldn't take my eyes off her. Unfortunately, she was married. Well she would be, wouldn't she?

Our eyes met and that wonderful chemistry took complete control. Wow! What she could see in me I just don't know. It was obvious to anyone with eyes that even half worked what I could see in her.

It wasn't long before she came down to visit me in

248

Hove and, to cut a long story short, she moved in a little while later. Not surprisingly, this didn't go down too well with either her ex-husband or her family. Her ex wanted to have me shot. Her father threatened to drown me. Her brother went to the local karate club and asked how long it would take for him to learn enough karate to be able to beat me up. The instructor, a certain Scotsman by the name of Phil Owen, who trained with me regularly, smiled at him nicely and said, 'Forget it, son. You'll never catch him up!'

As time passed, the husband accepted that Karen was never going back. Her brother and me became friends when he realised that I loved the ground she walked on, and that she loved me. Even her Dad said that he wanted to meet the man who had stolen his daughter's heart.

I was keen to meet him, too, but only when I was ready – it was going to be my timing, not his. So, the next couple of times I went to Inverness to teach I made a point of being too busy to see him. On the third trip I did arrange to visit, and I arrived at his door suited and booted.

I knocked and waited. The door was opened by a man who was equally well dressed. He invited me in. I said, 'Excuse me, Mr Fraser, but before I come over your threshold I want to clear the air.'

I explained to him that I hadn't intended to fall in love with his daughter, and that I regretted any pain I'd caused him and his family. I didn't, though, regret my relationship with Karen.

He said, 'That's fine, young man. Please come in.'

I went inside, confident that he was no longer planning to drown me in his bath. And I was right. I spent a lovely afternoon with Karen's parents. For the first hour, her Dad and me sat bolt upright in the lounge, making polite conversation while Karen and her Mum chatted in the kitchen. Then her Dad asked if I'd like a wee dram. Who was I to say no to such an offer?

After the fourth wee dram our ties were loosened and our postures were relaxed. By the end of the evening all formalities had disappeared and the house was filled with laughter.

With everything sorted in Inverness, Karen and me returned to Hove to continue our passionate and fiery relationship. You see, Karen had a temper that was the equal of mine, and, while it's true that like attracts like, it's equally true that like can fight with like. That's certainly how it was for us. Our life together was either ecstasy or hell – there was nothing in between.

Anyway, despite the occasional trips into hell, I adored having Karen with me and, as all couples do, we gradually created our own little world. We even had a nickname for each other. I called her 'Flat-faced Bastard' because, although she was stunningly attractive, she had a broad face and a tiny nose. She called me 'Saggy-arse Face' because I'm not stunningly attractive. God has given me a Size 5 head with Size 7 skin on it. In the early mornings the skin on my face doesn't seem to fit right and, if I've been on the vodka the night before, it can take an hour or two for everything to fall into place.

One evening I returned home from the *dojo* wondering what sort of welcome Karen had planned for me. We'd had a few words before I'd gone out, and I wasn't sure whether I was coming home to ecstasy or hell. As I opened the front door, I thought to myself, What happens now? Do I duck or do I fuck?

Karen greeted me with a beaming smile and said, 'Sit yourself down, your tea's ready.'

I said, 'Thanks,' and sat down in front of the TV.

A moment later, she brought me a large brandy. I thought, Things are looking good! Then my tea arrived on a little tray, which she put in my lap.

'Is everything OK?' she asked.

'It couldn't be better,' I said. 'Come and join me.'

Karen nodded. 'I'll do better than that.'

Fantastic! I thought, and my mind rushed in a very particular direction. Unfortunately, Karen's thoughts were going the opposite way. As I conjured up images of ecstasy, hell hit me right between the eyes. Actually, it was the plate with my tea on it. Karen simply grabbed it and pushed it into my face. I'd been taught by my Mum always to chew my food, but that's a bit tricky when it's all over your head!

Karen's mistake was in thinking that I couldn't respond with a glass in my hand, a tray in my lap and food in my face. Of course I could! The glass went up in the air, the tray flew off my lap and I pushed her up against the wall.

'Don't ever, ever do that to me again!' I said, with food clinging to my saggy-arse face.

Before she had chance to respond, poetic justice took control. A picture on the wall came loose and fell on her head. She staggered forwards, giggling as she did. I couldn't stop myself from joining in, her humour was as infectious as her temper. I hugged her and she hugged me back. We collapsed in fits of laughter and, by the end of night, we were both in ecstasy.

It wasn't just pictures that fell off the wall. One morning all the kitchen cupboards came tumbling down. The flat had been renovated recently and the wanker who'd done the work had clearly cut corners. The cupboards were filled with plates, glasses, all the usual stuff, so there was glass everywhere. As the cupboards crashed I heard Karen scream. I ran into the kitchen to see her standing in the middle of the floor, bare-footed, wearing only a towel, because she'd just come out of the bath. I was terrified that she'd cut herself to bits, so I scooped her up and carried her into the lounge. I looked to see what damage had been done, and realised that there was none. In my usual, caring way I said, 'It's lucky you're a flat-faced bastard, 'cos if any part of your face had stuck out it would have got knocked off!'

Chapter 56

'THAT REALLY IS GOODNIGHT!'

One night, I returned home from the *dojo* at about 10.30, poured myself a brandy and settled down, waiting for Karen to return from the night shift she was working at a local private hospital. I was looking forward to a nice, relaxed, cosy evening. That was not what I got. Instead of a few drinks and a kiss and cuddle, I got a loony in a phone box and a few hours in a police cell.

The instant Karen walked in it was obvious that something was wrong. She was as white as a ghost and close to tears. I asked her what had happened.

'A man's just come up to me on the street and felt my breasts,' she said, her voice shaking. 'I couldn't stop him.'

'What did he look like?'

'Like a white Mike Tyson, with a tattoo of a spider's web on his neck.'

'Where did it happen?'

'Just round the corner, next to the phone box.'

I was out of the flat like a shot. To be honest, I didn't think there was any chance of finding the guy, so you can imagine my surprise – and delight – when I saw him actually making a call in the phone box. He was exactly as Karen had described. He looked like a real handful, but I'd handled plenty of tough-looking guys before – and they never looked half as tough once I'd hit them. He was going to be just one more. He was a loony in a phone box who was about to get knocked out. He wouldn't even know what hit him! As I sprinted towards him, I was thinking, This is Christmas! And here comes your fuckin' present!

I pulled open the door to the phone box and, as I'd hoped, the loony spun round. I didn't say a word, I just unleashed a corker of a right hand – bang! – which caught him flush on the jaw. It was as close to a perfect punch as I've ever thrown. When I felt it land, I thought to myself, Game over! Now I'm going home to finish my brandy.

I didn't even stop to watch him fall. I just turned round to go back to Karen.

Big mistake!

The loony hadn't gone down. Not only hadn't he gone down, he hadn't even noticed that I'd hit him! He should have been unconscious, but before I'd taken one step he was flying through the air towards me like some crazy rugby player. He hit me in my chest and the pair of us went crashing over a low wall.

My shock lasted for a fraction of a second. As we flew through the air with his head on my chest, I grabbed hold of his hair and pulled it back hard, whipping my hips round and driving a cracking elbow shot right into his jaw. Even if I say so myself, it was a great technique. I used my hips so well that I actually spun right over and landed on top of him. I climbed to my feet thinking, That really is goodnight!

But it wasn't. We weren't even close to goodnight.

As I stood up and climbed over the wall, so did he. I'm sure you appreciate that people don't normally get up after I've clunked them. Well, not in a hurry, anyway. This guy had just taken two really big shots and was coming after me again as if nothing had happened. I was beginning to think that either something had gone wrong with my techniques or else I was fighting that knight from the Monty Python film who wouldn't give up no matter what you did to him. The guy was actually growling as he came towards me, which was bloody impressive, because his jaw was all over the place.

I said to myself, 'Time for business!' and kicked him so hard in the knee that you'd have heard it crack if you'd been standing on the other side of the road. He staggered and I kicked him flush in the groin. He fell to his knees, groaning. At last I was making an impression. Time, I thought, to make more of a lasting impact.

I pulled back, measured my shot, and kicked him full in the face. He went backwards and down. At that moment a police car pulled up. I don't know whether I was disappointed or relieved to see them, but I do know that I was having some serious doubts about my fighting ability.

Anyway, they handcuffed me and put me in the back of the car, then called an ambulance for him. What amazed me was that they handcuffed him as well. Why, I wondered, did they feel the need to do that? The ambulance arrived along with another police car. One policeman went with the loony in the ambulance, the other two policemen got in the car with me. They looked at me in the mirror, then looked at each other, then looked at me again. In the end, one of them turned round and said, 'Who the fuck are you?'

I shrugged. 'Why?'

'Because it normally takes eight of us to arrest him, that's why!'

It turned out that the guy was a well-known trouble-maker and drug user. The reason I'd had to work so hard to stop him was that he was out of his head on speed! Which, as far as I was concerned, was good news. It meant that I was still functioning normally. After all, if it took eight cops to control him I couldn't complain if it took me five shots to stop him, could I?

They drove me to the station, took a statement and locked me in a cell. After about an hour, the cell door opened and three big cops came in. I stood up, thinking they were there to give me a kicking.

I said, 'You'd better understand, the first one of you is going to get hurt real bad!'

The policeman nearest to me went, 'No! No! It's nothing like that. I know who you are and I just want to shake your hand.'

It turned out he was a third *dan* in Wado Ryu karate, and the other two trained as well. Once they'd heard I was in the cells, they'd decided it was a great opportunity to talk about karate. They did also tell me that the guy I'd hit had since escaped from the hospital. It seems he'd woken up, knocked out a nurse and the copper who was supposed to be guarding him – even though he was still handcuffed – and hobbled off into the night.

'We'll find him, though,' the cop said. 'Once the drugs wear off, he'll collapse in a gutter somewhere.'

Which he did. When he was readmitted to hospital, they found that he'd got a badly broken jaw, a broken nose, three broken ribs, a dislocated knee and a pair of bollocks the size of oranges! He was in hospital for three weeks, after which he spent two years inside for hitting the nurse and the policeman.

There's an interesting end to this story, because, eighteen months later, one of the policemen visited me to say that the guy had been released from prison and would be returning to the area.

'I don't think he'll remember you,' he said, 'mainly because of all the drugs he'd taken that night, but he has been known to use blades, so you'll need to watch out.'

I thought that was really nice. He didn't need to warn me and I certainly appreciated the information. I did some checking on my tattooed 'friend' and came to realise what an absolute nutter he was. He spent most of his time drugged up on the sort of stuff that makes you really strong and impervious to pain and, when he was in that state, he caused trouble that most people couldn't handle. Once, he was refused admission into a nightclub. The doormen knew who he was and told him that he wouldn't get in. He told them he would, and jumped straight through a large plate-glass window and onto the dance floor. He cut himself to bits, but in the fight that followed it still took five doormen to get him back outside.

While Karen couldn't have managed this particular loony, she was more than capable of looking after herself in more normal situations. Once, as she cycled home, she realised that a guy was trying to look up her skirt. She just punched him in the face as she went past.

I loved Karen for many reasons, but one of the main ones, when I think about it, is that she was a female version of me.

Chapter 57

JAPANESE SLIPPERS

In 1990 I heard that a group of *karateka* were planning to go to Japan to train on a *gasshuku* – a summer training camp – run by Yahara Sensei. Two of the group, Caesar Andrews and Michael James, had been before and had always said it would be great if I could go, too. It had been thirteen years since I'd been in Japan, and it seemed like a good time to go back for a week or two's training. Once I said I was interested the whole thing snowballed. Wherever I taught throughout the UK I spoke of my intention to train again with Yahara Sensei and people asked if they could join the group. In the end, twelve of us flew out to Japan. It was a great squad, that was more than equipped to cope with whatever came its way. Apart from Michael James and me, there were Aidan Trimble, Bob Waterhouse, Jeff Westgarth, Ronnie Ross, Phil Owen, Simon Oliver, Simon Staples, Andrew

Zolver, Roy Cudjoel and Bob Banboyne. I called us the Dirty Dozen.

Michael and I met with Yahara Sensei in a restaurant in Tokyo before the course began. He explained that he wouldn't be there for the first day and a half, and asked me to teach. That felt strange. I was back in Japan after all those years and now I was going to be teaching them. Yahara Sensei listed tons and tons of stuff that he wanted me to go through in just a handful of classes, then he excused himself and left.

Michael said, 'There's far too much for you to do there. How will you get through it all in such a short time?'

'I won't,' I replied. 'I'll teach what I want.'

And I did. I taught one move and one *kata* in a proper, structured way. When Yahara Sensei arrived he got feedback from one of his students about what we'd been doing, and was obviously pissed off that I hadn't taken any notice of what he'd said. Still, I knew I'd done a good job and, when he took over, I was able to get on with what I'd gone to Japan to do – train!

The Japanese *karateka* we were training with were all university students. While they all held black belts and were dangerous, they were essentially young lads – all much younger and far more inexperienced than anyone of the Dirty Dozen. Don't get me wrong, they all had the hearts of lions and demonstrated great spirit. But they were just no match for experienced, senior grades like us.

Interestingly, for most of the course, Yahara Sensei taught very few kicking techniques, so when we finally got the opportunity to spar we were very keen to start throwing our legs around. It was then that I began thinking of the poor university students as 'Japanese slippers', because every time I looked across at Aidan Trimble, who is one the world's greatest kickers, he'd got one on each foot.

At night we all ate dinner together. As I was the second most senior *karateka* present, I sat on Yahara Sensei's right side. The etiquette was very formal and regimented. No one was allowed to begin eating until Yahara Sensei did. When he left the room everyone had to stand. The problem was, with him gone I was the most senior person in the room and Aidan was next. So, whenever I stood up, so did all the Japanese. Once we'd got the hang of that, Aidan and I made sure that we left independently – just to keep the young men on their toes, as it were.

After dinner I always had two Japanese students follow me back to my room. Their job was to open the door for me, ensure that everything was all right, and demonstrate all the formal types of courtesy that, to be honest, I didn't need. I'd have been much happier if they'd just stayed with the others and enjoyed themselves. I did tell them to give me my keys and leave me alone, but they wouldn't have any of it. They'd been given their orders by Yahara Sensei and were very keen to follow them to the letter.

After a couple of nights of this, I lost my patience. I grabbed the keys, told them in an appropriate manner that I was more than capable of getting myself to bed, and walked off, leaving them, as I thought, to return to their friends. But, of course, I was wrong.

What I didn't know was that Aidan was in the corridor some way behind the two Japanese, and he saw everything that happened next. The two guys were clearly unsure about how to respond. After all, I was their senior and, therefore, should be obeyed. However, Yahara Sensei had given them clear instructions to look after me. By way of a compromise, I guess, they decided to follow me, quietly, at a distance.

So, there we all were, I was walking off ahead, they were creeping along behind me and Aidan was following them.

Now, the truth of the matter is that I'd needed to get rid of the two students because I was absolutely desperate to fart – and I didn't want to embarrass them by doing it in front of them. Once I was on my own – as I thought – I raised one leg and let rip.

All I heard from behind me was, 'Oss!' as the two Japanese stopped dead in their tracks and bowed. Beyond them, I heard Aidan squealing with laughter. As he said to me later, 'That was it! I knew you'd really made it when I saw that they even bowed to your farts!'

The course itself was held on an island called Hajijo-jima, off the coast of Tokyo. The placed we stayed in looked like a concentration camp and, in fact, it turned out that it had been a prisoner-of-war camp during World War II. Although we didn't take any prisoners during the training, and plenty of claret was spilled, we did get on very well with our Japanese counterparts outside of the *dojo*.

After the course we returned to Tokyo, where we stayed for a few days. Yahara Sensei told some students to show us around, and they were good hosts. One night we were all hungry and I decided that we ought to go the very nice restaurant I'd met Yahara Sensei in at the beginning of our visit. I didn't appreciate that this was a very popular and expensive place and, therefore, very difficult to get into. When we arrived outside the restaurant, I told the student who was looking after us that we wanted a table. He shook his head, saying, 'Yahara Sensei says that it is not possible to get in here.'

Unfortunately for him I wasn't in the mood to be told what I could or couldn't do. I said, 'Let's me and you walk round this corner, because I want to talk to you about this.'

Once we were on our own, I explained to him that, no matter what had been said previously, we were going into the restaurant. This time, thankfully, he agreed without a second's hesitation. I think the fact that my hand was twisting his bollocks might have helped him change his mind! We had a lovely meal. It's just one of many great memories I have of the time when the Dirty Dozen went training in Japan!

Chapter 58

THE BIBS COURSE

Have you ever seen the TV programme *The Last of the Summer Wine*? Well, the bibs course is like *The Last of the Summer Wine* for *karateka*! Originally there were five of us – Mick Dewey, Billy Higgins, Bob Rhodes, Aidan Trimble and me – and we decided to do a course together. We thought students would like it, and it would be a good excuse for a get-together and a drink.

The first course we organised ran for two full days in Nottingham. Although it was well attended, it wasn't a good earner, with five senior instructors splitting the money. The second course we did was for only one day and it still didn't pay. By then, though, we'd realised that we didn't need to do a course at all. As we all work at weekends we agreed to meet during the week, from Tuesday night to Thursday lunch, to do a bit of training, eat some good food, drink some excellent beer and wine and talk about the old days. Aidan had to drop out due to all his commitments and that left the four 'old' men, who'd all fought together in the England team in the 1970s and gone on to become senior instructors. When we organised the first bibs course in 1995 we didn't realise it was going to become an essential part of our calendars and that, over time, we'd all have to dress up for it.

We go to a different venue every year – always somewhere nice and calm such as Stratford-upon-Avon or Bath or Cheltenham, somewhere where we can be silly without the risk of trouble – and I thought it would be fun if we all wore a drinking bib (a T-shirt) with our name, the year and place on the front. Everyone thought that was a good idea, so we had our bibs made. Then I saw an old hat in an antique shop and, being under the influence at the time, I bought it for £10. The others all wanted their photos taken wearing my hat, so I said that everyone should accept a quest – to buy a hat for the next bibs course. That was when we decided to forget the training completely and just enjoy a nice, social time together. Once we'd all got our hats, we were obliged to go on a new quest and we agreed that we'd all have to buy a waistcoat to wear on the next year's course. As the years passed, the quests became more and more demanding.

Now when we meet we all wear hats, frilly shirts, bow ties, waistcoats, white gloves, cufflinks, armbands and fob watches and carry walking canes. We find a nice, quiet pub which we visit at lunchtime and tell the landlord how we're going to be dressed and behaving in the evening. We always arrive early and the night begins with me tapping my cane on the bar, saying, 'Barkeep, get us fine ale and serving wenches in fine order!'

All night long people stare, laugh at us, and ask permission to take our photos. I don't know why.

One night we were in a restaurant that had a moose's head on the wall. Just for fun, I hit it with a roundhouse kick. The next minute, Billy Higgins jumped up and head-butted it. He hit it so hard he knocked both its eyes out. Later that night, he was throwing chicken bones over his shoulder so enthusiastically they were in danger of landing in other people's food and I had to do some quick apologising to the other diners. When we left the restaurant all the staff lined up to usher us out. Our poor van driver was terrified as he watched four drunk seventh *dans* wearing frilly shirts throwing punches and kicks at each other as they crossed the car park!

The bibs course is one of the highlights of my year and, in case you're wondering, our latest quest is for us each to buy a violin case and cape.

Chapter 59

PAULA

I first saw Paula in Torquay at a course I did with Aidan Trimble. She was training there with her mate, Collete. I knew that she was a member of the KUGB national squad and I remember thinking to myself, Bloody hell, she's good! And she's pretty.

Still, I was too busy doing my stuff to think any more about her and, although we did chat briefly, it was only as part of a crowd when we all got together after training.

I did get a bit more time with her, though, at the course disco. We'd both had a bit to drink and I asked her to dance. We were doing OK until she tripped and fell. I tried to catch her, missed, and ended falling on top of her. Two large bouncers picked us both up and put us in a corner, where we sat, giggling, for quite a while.

We met again on another course I was giving and, after that, I invited her to a course I had booked in Plymouth.

That was when things took off. We agreed to have a couple of days away together, and spent a weekend in Stratford-upon-Avon.

Paula had just bought her own house in St Helens. She had a good job and her own car, and was committed to karate, training most nights of the week. She was also nearly twenty years younger than me. I was in my mid-forties while she only in her mid-twenties. To be truthful, I didn't think that I had much chance with her in terms of a long-term relationship. I just thought I was lucky to be spending time with this beautiful, talented, young woman. Even Enoeda Sensei once told me that he thought she was a special person. To me, she remains the most beautiful person I've ever met. She's honest, true, strong, level-headed, has her ego under control, and always looks on the positive side of things.

Needless to say, we had a great time in Stratford. We liked the same food. We loved socialising and we loved training. I realised that she was the most amazing woman I'd ever known. We became very close very quickly. Neither of us thought that our age difference was going to be a problem, apart from the fact that, if we were going to have kids, which was kind of the plan, it was likely that I wasn't going to be with them for as long as she was – especially given the way I was living. That frightened her, I think.

Paula moved down to Lancing, to live with me, at the start of 1997. She worked for the Inland Revenue for a while, but her dream was to become a sign-language interpreter. Her Mum had become progressively deaf as the result of an accident, so Paula enrolled them both on a sign-language course. Paula had a natural talent for it and now she is a professional interpreter. We moved her Mum down to the south coast to be near us, and everything was just very, very nice. We laughed all the time.

Although Paula trained with me, I never went to watch her compete. She fought both nationally and internationally, but I stayed away from all of it. I wouldn't have coped very well if I'd seen someone clump her – and she did take some terrible digs. She was what you'd call a 'straight-liner'. She just bowed and then flew straight at her opponent. You can't fight people like that without getting bashed in the face, so I worked with her to improve her balance and her angles.

I remember saying to Enoeda Sensei one night that I was seeing a girl who was in the KUGB.

'Who?' he asked.

'Paula White,' I told him.

He said, 'I knew it! I knew it! She has changed so much! Her karate is so much better now!' Then he looked at me for a moment and beamed. 'You – you Casanova!' he said, and roared with laughter.

For the first year or two of our relationship, my drinking didn't cause a problem. Paula liked a drink herself, and, I think, in her eyes I was just 'Fun-time Dave'. Eventually, though, it got out of hand and, like most alcoholics, I didn't want to admit to it.

A couple of things happened that still haunt me. The first was the day that Mum, Ben, Janice and Tracey came round and I'd drunk so much that I was out of it. Paula tried to tell them how big the problem was. They didn't believe her straightaway. I went upstairs, but I could still hear Paula working to convince them. I could hear everyone arguing and crying about me. In the end, I couldn't take it any more so I went for a walk. I drank half a bottle of vodka in twenty minutes, went back in and called them all a 'bunch of witches'. End of argument. Everyone agreed I had a problem and I promised the people I loved most that I'd stop drinking.

I did a pretty good job of it too, but a year later the second thing happened. Enoeda Sensei died unexpectedly in Japan – I'll tell you more about that in a minute – and, when I heard the news, I had the excuse I needed to go for it again. Fuck it! The truth is I was desperate for a drink.

I'd bought Paula a talking teddy bear, the sort you could programme to say certain things. I'd programmed it to say some of our personal little sayings. She was over the moon with it. When she went to work I thought to myself, Right! I'll have a little drink, then lie down and wait for her to come home again.

No chance! If you're an alcoholic you can't have one little drink and then have a rest. When Paula got back I was completely wrecked. She couldn't take it any more.

She still loved me – and I loved her – but she was terrified that my drinking would shorten my life, and she couldn't bear the thought of losing me that way. So she decided that she had to leave. It tore us both apart.

We did meet a few times afterwards, but it was just too painful. We agreed that the only sensible thing to do was to stay away from each other – to keep our distance. The problem for me was that, not only was she in my heart, it felt as if she was in every room of my home. I thought to myself, If I don't get out of this bloody place, I'll never get off the bottle. So I moved to Nottingham.

And that's all I've got to say about Paula. I have no outrageous stories to tell. It was just me and her. Just perfection. I met the perfect girl and I blew it. Well done, me! Typical silly bollocks.

Chapter 60

SPECIAL TIMES

I've had many special times in my life – I've shared quite a few of them with you – and, without exception, they have all been made special by the people involved. That's why I've told you so much about my family and friends, about the people I've been fortunate enough to share my time with, rather than concentrate on my karate training and the tournaments I've won. Anyway, you know as well as I do that it's the relationships we share that make our life special – and that's certainly how it's been for me.

As you've probably realised, some of my most special times have been with Enoeda Sensei. They weren't always in the *dojo*, though. From the mid-1980s onwards, if I had a question or a problem to do with karate, I'd always do my own research and then, if I still wasn't sure, I'd phone him and ask for his advice. He was always forthcoming.

Beyond that, starting at about the same time, Sensei, Mick Dewey and me would meet two or three times a year for dinner and a lovely chat. These were purely social occasions. We did talk about karate occasionally and, whenever the subject of karate politics came up, Sensei showed incredible foresight. I can't count the number of times he told us what was going to happen because of decisions someone had made – and he was always right! Most of the time, though, we talked about our families and our lives in general. Sensei was always concerned that we keep healthy, and remain true to our own, personal karate way. For Mick and me these were fabulous nights, and I know that Sensei really enjoyed them, too. He said to us, right at the beginning, 'We must keep this up – we are like brothers.'

I organised each meeting with the same precision that I arranged Sensei's visits to my Brighton *dojo*. I'd book us into a lovely London hotel. Mick would get the train up from Portsmouth. I'd drive up from Brighton. I'd make sure that Sensei's room was good enough, meet with Mick for some lunch and a couple of beers, then we'd both get suited and booted ready to meet the Boss.

We always met early, about 6.30 or 7 p.m., often in the Britannia Hotel in Grosvenor Square. Then we'd go down to the Shogun, the Britannia's outstanding Japanese restaurant. Enoeda Sensei said that the sushi chef was magnificent and, of course, as soon as he walked in they made a great fuss of him. We were looked after royally and, I have to say, it was the best Japanese food I've ever had.

When we'd finished our meal we'd go back to the hotel and have a couple of drinks at the bar. I'd tell a few jokes

– often miming the actions so that Sensei could understand what I was talking about – and he would say, 'You are a Cock-a-ney, a Cock-a-ney!' and laugh his wonderful, booming laugh, as I tried to explain Cockney rhyming slang and East End humour.

These were never big drinking sessions. Sensei would normally go to bed at about 10.30 or 11, and he'd be up and gone by the time Mick and me came down for breakfast the next morning. He was always an early riser and I asked him once where he went. He told me that he liked to train at a golf club that had a fitness centre and gym. He'd do some running on the machines, and some swimming and stretching. I remember he said that he liked to stand in the pool in karate stances, twisting from side to side, as he let the jets of water massage his body.

The last time the three of us met was in October 2002, and the strangest thing happened. We'd had our usual lovely evening out, and agreed to meet again either before Christmas or in January. I'd promised Sensei that I'd phone him to see which date would work better for him, and then he'd gone to bed early, as we knew he would. Mick and me both commented on how well he was looking, and had a final drink in the bar.

The next morning, when we came down, we were surprised to see Sensei sitting there, finishing his breakfast. We joined him, but it wasn't long before he was ready to go. He stood up, walked behind me, touched my shoulder a couple of times and said, 'Mick, you look after him!'

Then he just turned and walked away in his usual vibrant manner.

It was the last time I saw him alive.

I phoned him in November and he said that we'd have to meet in the new year, because he was going to Japan. I asked if everything was all right and he gave me his usual answer, 'Fine. Fine! No problem.'

It was some time later that I first heard the rumours that he had cancer. I called Cheiko, his secretary, and she told me that everything was OK. I made some more enquiries and heard that a friend of Sensei's had successfully undergone the same operation for the same problem, so he was confident that he would also be fine. It was a confidence that, I believe, he held right to the very end. It was a confidence that, for once in his life, was misplaced.

Enoeda Sensei died at 3.30 a.m. on 29 March 2003.

Chapter 61

'YOU'VE JUST GOT TO FIGHT'

I got a phone call later that day telling me that Enoeda Sensei had passed on.

I said, 'Don't be ridiculous.'

I'd been with this man since I was seventeen. He was like a surrogate Dad. I just couldn't believe someone that strong, that healthy, that vibrant and that dynamic could be taken away. It made me feel very, very vulnerable and very weak.

I lost it completely.

Then Richard La Plante phoned me from the States. 'Are you all right?' he asked.

I told him the truth. 'Not really.'

He said, 'Look, you've just got to fight through this. I know it's terrible for you, but remember what Enoeda Sensei has achieved and the legacy he's left. If the roots of where you come from are in Japan, then he was the trunk

276

and the power, and you are his branches. Don't let it die. Don't give up on it.'

A couple of weeks later I was asked to teach in a club in Orpington by a gentleman called Graham Richardson. All of Sensei's students from Marshall Street were there. I started the class the way we normally finish it, with what's called *moksu*. It's a time when we sit, in silence, just calming the mind.

I said to them, 'I don't know if I can do this class for you, but I'll try my best and if it doesn't work out please bear with me.'

Anyway, we started and it was great. Sensei's spirit came into the hall. I can't remember the number of times when I just wanted to cry and hug someone, but I got away with it and after the class everyone did give me a hug.

When I didn't want to cry any more, I spoke to Richard again. He said, 'Now, listen to me. You've got a lot to offer. It will be disrespectful to the memory of Enoeda Sensei if you don't go forward now.'

He was right and I did go forward. It's what Sensei would have wanted me to do.

Chapter 62

KARATE

*K*arate is the template I use to live. It is not my way of life, rather it's a code of how I want to live. As soon as karate becomes a way of life, you've lost it. You still have to have your own thoughts and beliefs. If you like, karate is the skeletal structure, but the muscle tissue is the individual.

I said to Enoeda Sensei very early on in my training, 'If I want to do karate do I have to become a Buddhist?'

He said, 'No, of course not. A Muslim does karate as a Muslim. A Jew does it as a Jew, a Christian as a Christian.'

For me, karate is a fighting method combined with a code of behaviour that begins and ends with respect and courtesy. A karate gi is a wonderful thing! You can be a surgeon, a lawyer, a bricklayer or a docker, but once you take your clothes off and put a gi on you're all the same.

What's the most important thing in karate?
Spirit.
Spirit first, technique second.

Chapter 63

LEGACY

I'm going to tell you now about why I left Mick's organisation and set up on my own. I'm also going to tell you about some of the very good people I've got around me and my plans for the future. I've left this until the end because this is where it seems to fit best.

In truth, I've been working my way up to it. This is not the easiest bit to write. I don't know why that is but, somehow, out of all the things I've shared with you, this feels the most personal.

When I told my family and my closest friends that I was writing this book some of them said, 'Be careful, Dave. You'll be leaving yourself open.'

I think they were concerned that I'd reveal too much about myself. Maybe I have, but I believe you can reveal the truth without dropping your guard, and that you can be honest without weakening your position. After all, nobody's perfect and I believe that to pretend you are is a sign of weakness. As I'm sure you've realised by now, I've never done things I've believed in by half-measures – and you know what I think about consequence. So here we go...

I was involved with SEKU, Mick's organisation, for nineteen years and, although I had no plans to start my own association, I did know that at some point I'd have to move on. I needed to explore and develop some avenues of the martial arts that I didn't think would be fair to do within SEKU. Which is not to say that I thought there was a problem in the organisation – far from it. Under Mick's leadership SEKU is doing some fantastic stuff. It always has and it always will. No, this was about what I needed to do and, inevitably, the day came when I wrote the hardest letter I've ever written. In this letter I explained to Mick why I had to move on, and resigned from my position as Technical Director.

It's important for me to say here that Mick Dewey was, and still is, the man I'd choose to have as an older brother. Our relationship goes back over thirty years – from the time Ray Fuller tricked us into kicking lumps off each other! He's made me part of his family, with his lovely wife, Maureen, and two children, Damon and Kerry, whom I've watched grow up.

Damon turned into a lovely young man, intelligent, athletic and as tall and wide as Mick. Tragically, he was struck down with MS a few years ago and that's affected his family greatly.

I have so many fond memories of Damon. I remember him as a young boy sitting on the doorstep wearing only his underpants, and then running to his Dad, crying, because the door had blown to and pinched his arse. I remember him coming home, sobbing, to change his trainers for his hardest shoes, because he'd been hit by an older boy and intended go back and kick him. I remember taking him for a spin round the block in my borrowed black Ferrari and being asked, 'Does this go as fast as a red Ferrari, Uncle Dave?'

I treasure these memories, even though now they always bring a tear to my eye. Sometimes life just isn't fair and I really hate it when I can't do anything to change things for the people I love.

Mick read my letter, told me that he was sad I had to leave and that he understood my reasons. We made it clear to each other that we wouldn't let anything or anyone get in the way of our personal relationship, and that remains the case.

After hearing that I'd left, quite a few people within SEKU said they'd be willing to follow my lead if I formed another association. They shared my vision and objectives, and had originally joined SEKU to train with me. It was only then that the idea of creating the Academy of Shotokan Karate developed.

As I said before, I like to think that like attracts like, but maybe I've just been lucky. The people around me, such as Jess Lavender, Jeff Westgarth, Simon Staples, Paul Herbert, Michael Hogan, Paul Walton, Simon Oliver, Juli Pops, Ian Gregory, Anna Parkin, Graham Palmer and Dean Straker, have helped me to create what, I believe, can become a platform for the future progress of the Academy.

As a teacher, I also believe that if I can't produce students who surpass me in ability and understanding then I've failed. And I think that, given the individuals within my organisation, and where I want to go with my own martial arts, I have a chance.

No, that's not right. I *know* I have a chance. I've already got some young people who are exceeding where I was at their age. A prime example is Simon Staples.

When I left Brighton to move to Nottingham, I passed my *dojo* on to Jess Lavender. You know how much that *dojo* meant to me, and you might think that it would have been difficult to pass it on. It wasn't. Jess is one of the most capable and intelligent martial artists I have ever met. He is also a true friend. That made it as easy as it could possibly be.

Jess, in turn, passed his *dojo* on to Simon, who'd been training with him since the age of eight. Now in his mid-thirties, with a wonderful wife and two young children, Simon is a truly great example of a martial artist, and I'm very proud to have assisted in his progress. If he is the type of person I leave behind, then the legacy I'd dearly love to create will have been achieved.

I'm pleased to say that the Academy of Shotokan Karate is growing and thriving, and is not limited to these shores. We even have a strong contingent in Canada, where I first taught in 1992. I return every year, and I love both the place and the people.

One of my proudest moments since setting up the academy was when Enoeda Sensei's wife attended our national championships, endorsing what I believe my teacher, her husband, would have wanted. I presented her with a photo of Sensei from the sixties that she had never seen before. It was a very emotional moment for both of us. I'm very proud still to have a strong relationship with her and her family. It is one that I will always honour.

In all honesty, it seems quite weird that a white belt who did twenty-one knife hand blocks and failed his first grading, who looked no further than getting his yellow belt, is now a seventh *dan*, in charge of his own organisation, and is looked on by some as their guide.

As a *karateka*, I've always recognised and understood my different stages of development. What I've never really understood is what other people see in me. Actually, that's true for all aspects of my life. I was taught by my Mum that the most important thing is how you think about yourself, not what others think about you. So, while I'm very grateful for the people out there who support me, I have to say that my view of me isn't always the same as theirs.

I am quite happy in some respects with the guy who looks back at me in the mirror. Actually, in some ways I'm quite proud. But the truth is, I'm also disappointed with many aspects of myself – especially the alcohol.

Still, no one's perfect, eh? I can be of use to my students, my family and my friends. They just have to take the good things I can offer, and ignore the rest. That's the best I can do. I hope they understand that...

And that's it. That's my life so far. Right now I'm feeling strong and things are OK. I still miss Enoeda Sensei constantly. And Paula? Well, I will love Paula always. She's special.

I feel that I still have much more to do and much more to give. There's a weight on me now because of the Academy. I've got to make that right and, since Enoeda

Sensei is dead, there's no one to ask any more. I've just got to justify what I do. And I can! I've been so well schooled in martial arts that I can justify anything and everything I teach. No problem. I'm stronger now than I've ever been in my entire life.

What remains true – what has been true throughout – is that I've been blessed to have the best family in the world, and I love them to bits. I've also got some great friends.

As for the alcohol, I take that one day at a time. If you are facing the same battle, remember that there are good people out there who can help us. For me, the disease is like your worst nightmare in a fight – it's the one you can never beat.

Sometimes in a conflict situation just a look will make the other person shy away. Other times you have to be a little stronger and use some force. Occasionally you have to dig deep and give it all you've got. This disease, though, is one you can never kill off. No matter what you do, even when you think you've got it beat, it can get back up and come at you. You have to stay vigilant, because just when you think you're safe it comes back to bite your arse. You have to make only one mistake and you're back at day one.

So I know I've got a real scrap on my hands – but so has it! Enoeda Sensei always told me, 'Never give up.' And I won't. I can be a nightmare, too, and no matter how many times the disease knocks me down, I'll keep getting up. The Japanese have a saying, 'Knocked down six times, get up seven.' The truth is, I learned that before I went to Japan. I'd been taught it even before Kato Sensei back-kicked me and put me on my arse when I was a white belt at Blackfriars. I learned it from my Mum. She'd already taught me that, no matter what the world throws at us, we can always find a reason to come back stronger than ever.

This life is our one chance to create a worthwhile legacy – and that, more than anything else, no matter what our own imperfections, is worth fighting for.

Happy days!

Dave

Chapter 64

FINAL WORDS: DAVE HAZARD – HOW OTHERS SEE HIM

'Considering his vocation and the pain he can inflict, the misinformed would say that Dave Hazard was a right nasty bastard. Yet I have never known a more fair, honest and level-headed man. He demands excellence, but nothing less than he would freely give of himself. He commands respect and gives total loyalty in return. If only some governments and businesses were run on the same principles.'

Jess Lavender, sixth *dan*

'I have known Dave Hazard for thirty years and life is never dull in his company. He can be volatile and dangerous, kind and generous. When it comes to fighting he has few equals but it is as a teacher that he truly excels. An inspirational instructor, he is dynamic and effective in action, down to earth yet thought-provoking, and intelligent in communication of his ideas and techniques; he will incorporate anything that works from other disciplines into his karate. I am proud to call him my Sensei and my friend.'

Ronnie Ross, sixth *dan*

'Hazard. The name says it all. He's sort of Bruce Lee, Steve McQueen and Master Po rolled into one. Amazingly, he's still alive. I count myself lucky to have survived his lessons, shared his whisky, his laughter and his friendship for twenty five years.'

Richard La Plante, third *dan*, qualified boxing coach, psychiatric counsellor, author

I'd been training in Shotokan karate for seventeen years when Sensei Hazard came along and made me question what I'd been doing. Twenty-four years later and it's never been the same since. I am pleased to call Dave Hazard my Sensei, my mentor and my friend. He is a gentleman – and he still has the edge.'

Jeff Westgarth, sixth *dan*

'The two words that best describe Dave Hazard are loyal and honest. He is loyal to his family and friends, to his Sensei and his students, to those he loves and to those he once loved. Above all else, he's loyal to the truth. His karate is so honest and real it fizzes with commitment and promise – and, when he makes a promise, it's a guarantee. He's so committed to the truth that he'll tell it even if it hurts; that's how strong he is. With Dave Hazard there is no bullshit. He is, quite simply, a *real* inspiration.

Chris Parker, author, martial artist

'When the average man is thinking what to do, Dave Hazard has said it, done it and gone! He's an inspiration to train with, painful to fight and enjoyable to be around. He's the real deal.'

Aidan Trimble, seventh *dan*, former world champion

'Who is Dave Hazard? Well, to many he is a dynamic and inspirational man. He is honest and fair. He is not always the easiest person to be around, but he is always the first to help when you need it. He has a devilish sense of humour, and is also annoyingly early for everything. He can be astonishingly forceful one minute and incredibly gentle the next.

Who is Dave Hazard? He's the one who makes our Mum's eyes shine. He's my brother.'

Janice Hazard